I0556426

2015

Groundwaters

"Bubbling up in our own good time"

After a Spring Shower. *Photo by 14-year-old Christine Thom*

Produced by the Staff of

Groundwaters Publishing, LLC

Pat Edwards, Managing Editor
Jennifer Chambers, Editor
Patrice Broome, Copy Editor
Jim Burnett, Sr., Business Manager

Copyright © 2015
by *Groundwaters* Publishing, LLC

All rights reserved.
No part of the material protected by this copyright
notice may be reproduced or
utilized in any form or by any means, electronic or mechanical,
including photocopying,
recording or by any informational storage and
retrieval system
without written permission
from the copyright owner.

ISBN-10: 0996426124
ISBN-13: 978-0-9964261-2-1

First Edition, October 2015

Published by
Groundwaters Publishing, LLC

P.O. Box 50, Lorane, Oregon 97451
http://www.groundwaterspublishing.com

About the Cover photo: a public domain posting by "Tidy" on Pixabay.com

Groundwaters

Introduction

For those who aren't familiar with *Groundwaters*, it is a 32-page literary quarterly that was published and distributed free throughout Lane County, Oregon for over 10 years. Because the high cost to produce each issue outdistanced the resources at hand, the last quarterly was published in January 2015.

From 2008 to 2015, it was published under the auspices of the non-profit "The *Groundwaters* Magazine Project" under the 501(c)(3) umbrella of the Applegate Regional Theater, Inc. of Veneta, Oregon and was staffed by four volunteer editors: Pat Edwards, Jennifer Chambers, Pat Broome and Jim Burnett, Sr. Before 2008, it was published by its founders, Judy and Sonny Hays-Eberts who set it up to honor "community" – the West Lane County community, to be specific, and, to a large degree, it still does.

When the magazine changed hands, its focus became to honor local writers and poets. We especially wanted to encourage amateur, "kitchen table" writers, to share their talent with our readers. We were soon humbled by the degree and quality of local unpublished writing talent that was waiting to be shared. For each issue, 600-700 copies were produced and distributed and our contributor base grew.

Many of our regular contributors soon began to pick up followers and some have even been encouraged to self-publish their work. Most, however, are content to have their work read and appreciated in the pages of *Groundwaters*.

Joining them occasionally were the stories, essays, memoirs and poems of some of Lane County's most recognizable authors and poets. By allowing their works to be published alongside fledgling authors and poets, they brought acceptance and a degree of respect to not only the magazine, but to the amateur writers, as well. We felt it especially important to honor the work of those under eighteen, and our section called "Bubbling Up" has been devoted to that age group. We have been able to feature many talented young writers and artists, some of whom have gone on to have commercially-published work as they have grown.

Our work with youth in the magazine morphed into an outreach program that was designed by Jennifer Chambers and funded by the Oregon Country Fair's Bill Wooten Endowment Fund for several years. Through this school outreach program, we were able to publish two chapbooks and seven paperback books authored by students at Lorane Elementary School (two chapbooks of comic strips from a workshop given by Nick DeAngelo) and Veneta Elementary School in which the students' writing and artwork were featured. We hope to continue this project at some point. The autograph parties that were held at VES were so much fun to witness!

A few of our authors and poets, like their writing styles, are works in progress. We frequently see the efforts they make to improve and learn by joining writers' groups and asking friends, relatives and members of the *Groundwaters'* staff to proofread their stories and poems. As their confidence grows, in most cases, so does the quality of their writing. It is that growth and confidence that we want to encourage and instill in each one, if possible.

All of our writers, regardless of their skill levels, have something to say – a story to tell – in their own way and style. Our goal is to enable the less-experienced to do so in the best way possible.

So, this is the first of what we propose to be a series of yearly "issues." The stories and poetry are similar to those that you would find in any of our previous issues – there's just more of them. The book is smaller in size than the magazine, which was 8½" x 11", and it is now organized by sections – fiction, non-fiction and poetry – instead of being all mixed together, but the content is from your favorite authors and poets, and some new ones, as well. Our concept was to take a whole year's worth of material and put it into one book. We weren't sure our writers would transition with us – but they have done so, emphatically.

Check out our submission guidelines in the back of the book; they include the next deadline for submissions. We are no longer assigning themes to issues as we did with the quarterlies, but if there is a strong request for them, we can always bring them back. In the index, we have a complete list of the contributors for this issue, and if you go to the "From the Bookshelf" section, you'll see what books are now available from each of our writers who have published in the last few years.

Even better, purchase a copy of the books that interest you and help us honor our local talent!

We look forward to this new era of *Groundwaters* and remain grateful to the writers, artists, poets, word-painters and advertisers who have been with us over the years.

Here's to many more issues!

To Our Faithful Advertisers Over the Years...

Blue Rooster Inn Bed & Breakfast

An historic Oregon farmhouse on 67 scenic acres

82782 Territorial Rd
Eugene, OR 97405
(541) 684-3923   http://www.blueroosterbnb.com
Nancy Pelton, Owner

THE OUT BACK GARAGE **BY APPOINTMENT**

Foreign • Domestic • Light Trucks

Shop	541-942-8342	79604 Fire Road
Ken	541-520-1777	PO Box 177
Jim	541-554-6040	Lorane, OR 97451

theoutbackgarage@live.com

Elan Realty

Getting You Results In Real Estate......
Is Our Business!!!

541-225-8809 (cell)
541-225-5167 (fax)
glorias0104@aol.com
http://www.elanrealty.net
1146 Park Ave. Eugene, OR 97404

Gloria Edwards
Principal Broker Owner

Jim and Pat Edwards'

Lorane Family Store

80301 Territorial Rd.
Lorane, OR 97451
(541) 942-5711 / (541) 942-0573 fax

Featuring
From Sawdust and Cider to Wine
http://www.sawdustandcider.com

KNEE DEEP CATTLE COMPANY
FREE RANGE GRASSFED BEEF

3S

Locker Beef
Oregon Bred & Raised
No added hormones or antibiotics
USDA inspected

541-345-0685
http://kneedeepcattlecompany.com/

and...

• Alix Mosieur
• Blue Swan Galleries
• Chuck McJunkin Well-drilling
• Handyman Construction
• Judie Brantley
• LeRoost Lorane
• Robbie's Window-box Caffe
• Stillpoint Farm
• Winter Green Farm

Buying or Selling in Lane County?

Sharon Can Help!

Sharon Malcolm has nearly 20 years experience helping people buy and sell in Greater Lane County. She has earned many accolades for her sales record, but finds the greatest reward is seeing her clients achieve the results they're hoping for!

Call Sharon at
(541) 484-2022
(541) 517-8222 (cell)
sharonmmalcolm@aol.com

Windermere
REAL ESTATE
BROKER
ABR, CRS, GRI

FARM STORE & MUCH MORE

*Livestock Feed	*Alfalfa, Hay & Straw
*Pet Foods & Supplies	*Veterinary Supplies
*New & Used Tack	*Grooming Supplies
*Carhartt Clothing	*Wrangler Western Wear
*Montana Silver Jewelry	*Western Gifts & Cards
*Wood Fuel Pellets	*Propane
*Landscape Products	*Garden Plants & Supplies

Since 1994

The **FARM STORE**
87774 TERRITORIAL ROAD
VENETA, OR.
935-3604
Open Mon-Sat 8:30-6:30

Owners
Roger, Vicky
& Travis
Soverns

Thank you for your support!!

The Philosopher's Corner

Thinking outside the box

By Jimminy Cricket

LEGEND, One Perspective
By Jim Burnett (aka Jimminy Cricket)

It seems to me that we are rapidly losing our sense of legends. Legend: a story interwoven with fact and fiction, long ago reality and imagination interwoven and passed down through generations of story-tellers and wisdom teachers.

The times, they are a-changin... Familiar legends fade into the shadows cast by urban legends – mere snippets circulating round and round the Internet and forwarded from email box to email box.

Legends of old generally served a good purpose; they were thinly disguised morality tales. Urban legends, birthed from a new purpose, are meant to fool the naive, to mislead, to misinform and misdirect. The underlying energy is sometimes viciously political; sometimes malicious; and often overlays truth with base fiction, attacking someone's character, reputation and more.

Other urban legends spew forth other types of fiction – warnings contrived to misinform by deliberately circulating false warnings of imminent danger to computer or livelihood.

Some urban legend makers do it for the thrill of seeing their creations circulate the planet. they compete to see whose email or post will "travel" the farthest and last the longest. Others of these tricksters have turned urban legends into a multi-million dollar industry. Their efforts are most evident in highly-charged political seasons, serving to reinvent political candidates.

What will tomorrow's legends consist of? Something better, I hope. Will there be a return of legends like that of Robin Hood, King Arthur and the like?

I hope so.

Our own Jim Burnett, Sr. (aka Jimminy Cricket) has been with *Groundwaters* since it changed hands in 2008. He's guided us through the incorporation process and the setting up of the non-profit "The *Groundwaters* Magazine Project." Jim lives in Portland, Oregon with his wife Jonni and just happens to be Pat Edwards' "big brother" and major supporter.

Photo Gallery

Table of Contents

(There are a few instances where alphabetical order is not strictly adhered to)

POETRY

BUBBLING UP POETRY (Young Writers' Section)

COMIC STRIP

OUR CONTRIBUTORS

FROM THE BOOKSHELF

Note: Some authors have more books than are listed here. This is just a sampling of the more recent ones)

GUIDELINES FOR NEXT YEAR'S ISSUE

Photo Gallery

The Tranquility of Youth. Sixteen-year-old Pat Edwards on her horse Rocket on their farm near Lebanon, Oregon (1959). *Photo by Barbara Smith Isborn*

Groundwaters

Fiction

Fiction

Table of Contents

Down in the Dump
By Mary Alexander

L orinda, whenever are you going to get that garbage to the dump? It's starting to smell bad and I'm afraid that javelina herd is going to raid it. They could hurt the dogs."

"Mom, I knowI know! It will have to wait until Saturday. I can't take any more time off from work and the land fill gate closes before I can get there on weekdays."

We live on ten desert acres on the edge of nowhere, without city services, so my unpaid second job is sanitation engineer and all-purpose ranch hand for our two dogs, pet horse, a desert tortoise, and assorted doves.

My sixty-eight year old Mom has been a "grass" widow since I was eighteen and Dad left us for his office intern. I've been a "grass" widow since I was thirty-eight and turned out to pasture when my ex took a fancy to the young carpenter who built our patio deck. They came out together and moved to Haight Ashbury.

Living in the boondocks isn't just beautiful sunsets and quiet serenity. So on Saturdays, I load up the accumulated bags of garbage, after composting what's compostable, and other trash, what's left behind by trespassers passing through our property. Then, two times a month I haul them in my pickup to the county landfill. That's what Mom was on my case about. I missed the last regular haul when I took the dogs to the vet after they lost a battle with cholla cactus when they chased a jackrabbit into its burrow. Cholla is unforgiving. The pernicious hooked needles have to be pulled one by one from unhappy canines who need minor sedation for the painful process.

Saturday arrived. In my sweat-soaked grubbies I finally had the Ford Ranger loaded up and on my way to the landfill. It's fourteen bucks for each load, which I'd gladly pay someone else to transport the awful offal, but there are no takers. I passed through the gate and paid the fee at the weigh station. The gatekeeper directed me to the familiar area for offloading. It was getting late in the afternoon. I was really anxious to get home and into a warm shower to relieve my aching muscles. As I backed up to the edge of the dump site embankment, I noticed that the only activity, other than the scavenging black ravens, was where the workmen were bulldozing dirt on the far side of the huge area. It was surprisingly quiet for a Saturday, and I was the only one on this side.

I pulled on the safety brake before getting out of the cab. Grabbing the long-handled shovel off the top of the load, I went around to the tailgate to let it down. I glanced at the steep embankment and thought I almost got too close. Seconds later that thought came back to bite me. I pulled down the tailgate and took a flier straight down the eight foot cliff into the stinkiest garbage imaginable. Even the ravens had decided it was too rotten to bother with.

Nothing was broken except my dignity. I tried to stand up, but kept slipping and sliding into more ugly goo. Of course, I had left the shovel leaning against the truck fender before lowering the tailgate. I tried to pull myself up the bank but the soil was too porous. I couldn't get a good grip and it kept crumbling under me.

That's when I started yelling for help. My cries brought a few curious crows and, way overhead, one hawk. I suppose I yelled for ten minutes. It seemed like half an hour. The sun was lower in the west than when I'd arrived. That's when I sank into the dirt I'd pulled down and began to cry. Am I to be stuck here overnight? God help me, it's a weekend. This place is closed tomorrow. I'll be vulture brunch by Monday!

Back at the weigh station the gatekeeper was looking at his watch, "I wonder where that dame is who came in the Ranger? She better clear out pretty soon. I promised Vera I'd be home on time tonight."

"Hey, Gabe, you all done for tonight? Did you see anything of a woman in a Ford Ranger with a load?"

"Naw. We were way over on the far side all afternoon. What're you sayin'? Did you lose one?"

"Well, I'm beginning to think so. She should have been finished unloading and out by now. I shouldn't leave the booth. Would you mind hiking over that way and see what's going on with her?"

"Okay. Reynaldo's giving me a ride home, so don't let him leave without me. He should be along in a few minutes."

Gabe quickly covered the quarter mile distance around the site and spotted the Ranger at the precipice. As he approached, he heard the *mournful wail of a downhearted frail*, just like in the old Frank Sinatra song, "Birth of the Blues"

"Good God, lady, what are you doing down there!"

My savior arrived! The tears kept dripping, but now they were from relief. I was not going to spend the night in this sewage after all.

When his question penetrated my brain, sarcasm took over. "What does it look like? I'm taking a garbage bath! I fell, of course, and I can't get out of here. Help me, pulleease!"

"Well, gee, I don't know. I can't reach you without falling in myself."

I said, "The shovel... get the shovel and lower it so I can grab it."

He did, but it wasn't nearly long enough. "You'll have to bring a ladder. Make sure it's long enough."

"Lady, what's your name?"

"Lorinda."

"Well, Lorinda, we don't have a ladder. We've never had a reason to keep one around. I'll have to get one of the guys to call the fire department to bring one."

"Oh, don't leave me here. It's getting dark. Please don't leave me." By this time I was humbled and no longer sarcastic.

"Lorinda, don't worry. I'll only be a little while to get to a phone, and I'll come right back, I promise."

~~*~*~*

He kept his promise, but he said it might take a while for the firemen to bring the ladder because they were off on a fire call at the moment.

He said, "While we are waiting, if you can move over a few feet, I'll go ahead and unload your truck. At least you'll have that taken care of when we get you out."

I guess I was whimpering a bit when I thanked him and struggled to get out of my immediate slime into nearby slime and stuff.

"Don't feel bad, Lorinda. I bet you'll laugh about this tomorrow. Okay, maybe not tomorrow, but this time next year."

I asked, "What's your name? I can't always call you 'My Rescuer' when I tell this story."

"I'm Gabe, that's short for Gabriel. Mom said I was her 'little angel' until I started raising hell in my teens."

This guy had the instincts of a therapist. I needed a reason to smile right then.

He threw the bags and trash over the cliff and was stowing the shovel when another fellow drove up in an SUV. He leaned out the driver window and called, "Hey, Gabe, I really got to get home. My kid's got a soccer game in an hour."

Gabe replied, "You can't just leave me here, Ray. How am I going to get home?"

"Pete's still at the gate, waitin' for the firemen. Maybe he can give you a lift. I gotta go. See you Monday." Ray took off.

"Gabe," I called up, "if I get out of here I'll give you a ride. Just let me know where you need to go."

"When you get out, not if. It's a deal, but it's gonna be a little hard to explain you to my wife. How come your husband isn't doing this hauling bit? It ain't usual to see ladies out here."

"He hauled himself away years ago. I'm alone now."

"So's my brother Rick. He's been batching it for too long. You should meet him."

"I hope he isn't at your house now. I sure wouldn't want to meet him smelling like this."

Gabe bantered like that for the two hours we waited for the firemen to bring a ladder. It was fully dark when they finally came. They let me use some water from their drinking Igloo to wash my hands and get some of the muck off my shoes. They offered me a small canvas tarp to sit on so I didn't soil the seat upholstery in my truck.

Gabe lived about five miles from the landfill, but it was in the direction opposite of where I'd be going home. He introduced me to his wife when I dropped him off, and had her take down my number so he could give it to his brother Rick.

I finally made it home around eight o'clock. Mom ran out to meet me as I pulled into my driveway. "Good heavens, Lorinda, I've been out of my mind with worry. Whatever happened to keep you so late? Oh, you smell awful! Where have you been?"

"I've been down in the dump, Mom, just down in the dump."

Photo Gallery

The Henry Siblings, ca 1922, in Hibbing, MN contributed by author, John Henry. "My father, Jim Henry, is the middle child, his sister Elvera is on the right and brother Marion is on the left."

Koby the Toad

(an alternate tale of the Jersey Devil)

By D.J. Barber

Koby the Toad lived in a mostly dry-rotted stump behind the small cabin home of Mrs. Leeds. The cabin lay deep in the Piney Woods by a blackwater stream just north of Great Bay. Toby had a happy life in the sandy soil of the Piney Woods and was under no illusions of being some rich prince under an evil spell from which a kiss from a lovely maiden might free him to a princely life.

No – Koby the Toad was quite content with life as it was. His neighbor, Mrs. Leeds', life, was not as carefree as Koby's. She had married young, and to a foolish brute of a man who kept his poor missus in a state of abject poverty. When their first child was born, it was said that he wasn't the handsomest of children – and sadly – the second-born, a daughter, was a bit less handsome. The years tumbled by and the progeny of the Leeds' grew, with each succeeding child a bit less, shall we say, attractive.

Mrs. Leeds' last child, her thirteenth, was that legendary horror that stalks the Piney Woods, even unto this day! It was said that Mrs. Leeds, in the agony of her birth pangs, cursed the poor thing – and when it was born, it jumped from her womb – through a window of the small cabin, and then bounded into the deep forest that surrounded all.

Koby was witness to these things and his hope was that the horror – a devilish creature indeed – would not grow to maturity by feeding on toads!

Koby leapt around to and fro from his stump to the Leeds' back window and back again, sipping from a puddle by the cabin and catching the odd bug or two for his supper.

Mister Leeds was a woodcutter and a drunkard. Sometime after the birth of his thirteenth, while in one of his foul moods of anger, he stumbled and fell into the blackwater stream and drowned. His cries for help fell on over two dozen deaf ears—all deaf to his voice, and so the mean-spirited Mr. Leeds was no more a threat to the many children or Mrs. Leeds.

The elder ugly children of Mrs. Leeds took up the woodcutting tasks previously done by her mister, and, for a time, Mrs. Leeds led a happier life. Koby the Toad would catch a smile on her drawn face from time-to-time. But it seems that happy times are oft fleeting ones.

Some months after the death of her mister, Mrs. Leeds' thirteenth child returned to the small cabin by the blackwater stream. And night after night, the last-born of Mrs. Leeds would come in the late darkness and steal away one of its siblings into the deep Piney Woods' recesses – thus its legend grew!

Mrs. Leeds was soon all alone again, except for her small, wart-covered neighbor who lived in the mostly dry-rotted stump behind her cabin.

Now the mostly dry-rotted stump took some damage over the following winter and Koby the Toad determined he might well indeed have to move, and so he fixed his eye upon a crevice underneath Mrs. Leeds' cabin. Having little in material possessions, his move was quick and easy. His new home under the small cabin was found to have spacious accommodations for one as diminutive as Koby. There was a spider or two, but Koby soon made a meal of them and then got around to settling in to his new home.

Some years later, the old woman transformed – her once olive complexion was now decidedly green; her once noble nose was now a long hook with a wart on it of which Koby could be proud. She continued to dress in black garb, including a wide brimmed black hat, in deference to her long lost mister. She had earned her the reputation of being a black witch.

The villagers from over by Little Bay were uneasy in Mrs. Leeds' presence and soon asked her to take herself and her business affairs elsewhere. Her pleas of innocence fell on deaf ears, much as her mister's pleas for help had so many a year before. She cursed them all with a venomous snarl, telling them that her thirteenth child would seek her vengeance upon them all!

Sadly, this last discourse only reinforced her image as a black witch.

Meanwhile, back at the cabin, Koby the Toad had been running around in circles trying to avoid old Sam the Snake, who had blundered underneath the cabin, in search of a place to take a nap during the heat of the day. But now he thought maybe he might make a meal of Koby the Toad!

Koby hopped from under the cabin and made a beeline for his former digs in the now entirely dry-rotted stump. Sam the Snake had Koby cornered and was about to strike when that old broom of Mrs. Leeds struck him square on his triangular head. Koby the Toad saw her standing above snarling at the snake as he slithered off into the nearby pines and brambles. Never a lovelier sight had he ever beheld in all his days!

Mrs. Leeds walked in a huff back to her small cabin, swearing snake curses, and Koby the Toad followed after, his heart aflutter. He leapt inside the cabin just as she slammed the door and found a place by the old woodstove in the kitchen where he might worship her from afar.

He suddenly realized what a fright he must look. He had, after all, just avoided being old Sam's afternoon snack – and by crawling through the ruins of his former home he must look simply terrible. And so he departed through the broken baseboard behind the woodstove and underneath the small cabin. He exited through the crevice behind and hopped over and into the blackwater stream to take a short swim. He hopped up on the bank and, with a brave heart, hippity-hopped to the front door of Mrs. Leeds' small cabin.

He knocked by leaping against the door a few times and after a minute she answered, looked to and fro, and slammed the door, but not before Koby the Toad hopped inside. She turned about, not noticing him, and returned to the large, black cauldron in the fireplace.

Koby the Toad sat by the side of the woodstove, entranced, and watched as Mrs. Leeds softly chanted as she stirred a large ladle in the great black cauldron. She spoke of cat's livers and salamanders – quail eggs and lizard tongues. He blinked and smiled as she set a cup on a shelf after taking a sip of tea. And then she continued to, aaah, stir the pot, as it were.

Mrs. Leeds turned from the cauldron and scampered into the kitchen, nearly stepping unawares on Koby, and returned with a few small bottles. She set them down and picked up the smallest and opened it up, pouring its entire contents into the brew. She then went back to stirring. Her chanting soon continued: "...rat's eyes and ground chalk, peppercorns and frog eggs..."

She toiled late into the night.

Then, 'round about two-thirty in the morning, Mrs. Leeds let forth a small squeal! It seems she had hit a snag – a missing, but key ingredient in her slow-cooking brew! She ran to a shelf and grabbed a large and dusty journal. Flipping through page after page, fingers sliding down and down again, she came upon her absent component – the right front leg of a toad!

She whirled around, a grim sneer on her green face, at the recent memory of whacking that black snake with her broom. For under the ruins of that old hickory stump behind the cabin, she remembered clearly the little warty toad that had presumably been the snake's quarry. She flew from her journal and jumped out the front door. Running around to the back she pawed through the crumbling mass of dry-rotted wood in search of Koby the Toad.

Our small friend crept back behind the woodstove, fear now enveloped his toady mind for his dilemma was if he now showed himself, his own true love might well take his life – and all for a relatively small and insignificant right front leg. If it were a back leg – either one – well, that would be simple – he would just hop off and forget, painful as it might be, his newfound heart's delight.

However – his right front leg, which he used mainly for leaning on, since he was left-handed – might well be a token gift that would express his true love for the black-clad widow of the drowned woodcutter, Leeds. The problem was, she just might accept the offer of the front right leg and throw the rest away – much like the proverbial baby with the bathwater! Now a love-hate relationship was attractive in many ways, but a love-fear relationship was untenable – how can one hop in two directions at the same time?

And so Koby the Toad sat and thought while Mrs. Leeds ran to and fro cursing the world for lack of one toad!

It may have been the entire racket she raised, or perhaps just the late night hour, but suddenly and without warning, Mrs. Leeds' thirteenth child burst through the door of the small cabin by the blackwater stream. It was a curious sight to the eye of Koby the Toad; for although this creature was a fearsome and horrible sight, it did bear a striking resemblance to Mrs. Leeds. Yes, even through the fish-scale skin and the yellow owl's eyes, the legs of a bull – right down to the hawkish nose and olive-green complexion, this was its mother's child! And in its outstretched hand, more like an eagle's talons, the beast held a small object in offering to its dear mother.

She advanced slowly, looking at this horrid creature in a manner only a mother's love could explain. She reached out and took the gift from her only surviving child and watched as it turned about and was gone as fast as it had come.

Mrs. Leeds took what was given her and tossed it in the cauldron; and with her large paddle she began, once again, to stir and softly chant. But in that moment – that singular moment while her hand was still above the bubbling gruel – Koby the Toad saw that what was tossed in was nothing less than the right front leg of a toad.

In his utter happiness he hopped out from under the woodstove, and in his loudest and best voice, sang out in a deep croak.

Mrs. Leeds, for her part, turned about and upon seeing Koby the Toad, shouted with a scream of the most horrid anger ever heard before upon the Earth and, perhaps, even in the Heavens. She sprang to the spot where a startled little Koby the Toad sat, lifted her black leather shoe, and tried to stomp Koby the Toad into dust. He smartly retreated behind the woodstove and escaped through the little hole in the baseboard.

Koby the Toad departed the Piney Woods that very night. He hippity-hopped across acres of forested lands until he came to Great Bay and there he found a place under an old, abandoned crabbing boat and lived out his days, dieting on flies and a little sand flea or two. His love for Mrs. Leeds remained intact for all his remaining days – his fear of her did as well.

The legend of Mrs. Leeds' Thirteenth child grew and grew, but towards that horrid thing Koby the Toad could hold no animus because from time-to-time Koby the Toad would spy the devilish creature prowling on a hunt. Koby was forever grateful that the beast chose not toads as a snack. Its green complexion and hooked nose was a reminder to Koby the Toad of happier days beneath a small cabin that sat beside a blackwater stream deep in the Piney Woods, and a common bond that the creature held an unreturned love for the same one as he.

The Art of Love
By John Henry

*"The more I think it over, I feel that there is nothing more
truly artistic than to love people."* – Vincent Van Gogh
*"Teams that go through the playoffs, you know, (don't) paint a Picasso
every time they play."* – Tampa Bay Lighting coach Jon Cooper

Eric was a three-time loser. The last time he hedged his bets and got his lawyer friend to draw up a pre-nuptial agreement which Doris refused to even consider. So it cost him a few million more from that mistake than the two others. Doris didn't take him to the cleaners as much as have him pay premium for her services as the trophy wife. He had put her on a pedestal, and connected to her like one does to abstract art.

Eric wasn't jaded. He complained to his golf buddies about all women being self-serving entrepreneurs, not prostitutes, just in the same business as himself and his friends. The profit motive stirs the pot and you can't dislike someone for taking advantage of an opportunity to enrich themselves.

At least Doris didn't surprise him with a child, like wife number two. Alicia was a tempestuous beauty. She was a starlet in Eric's real estate business, a go-getter, a sales magnet. On Eric's part is was a hormonal fling. He was breaking one of his cardinal rules, "Don't fraternize with the help," but Alicia was seductive in her assertive way. She gave him two terrific kids and made him more money than it cost him when she left the marriage. She was a whiz at business and was CEO and part owner of Eric's manufacturing operation in Cleveland. They continue to have a terrific business relationship and the kids are great assets.

The first wife was Jessica. She was too beautiful for her own good. Eric got in line to take her out. She was not only beautiful but brilliant. She was majoring in music and creative writing, acting with the university theater company, and busking on weekends to support her college expenses. Eric thrives on upgrading the product. He loves the diamond in the rough, the mismanaged patent, the failing real estate project that needs tweaking. Eric found that Jessica was nearly perfect. She could be in the Louve if she was a sculpture, she'd win an Oscar with the right direction, and she'd have a platinum album with the right producer. She was a raw gem needing faceting and polishing.

Dating Jessica was hard work; the competition was ferocious. Eric was getting a second engineering degree and his research into computers was consuming him almost as much as this new girl friend. He saw his research as a million dollar science project and Jessica as the fulfillment of his softer, artistic side. Eric put his energies into what would profit him the most – his computer research, his degree, and Jessica.

Jessica's parents were working class drones. She was deprived of the refined aspects of the good life. In college and through the arts, she was learning about how the other half lived; but down deep, she was a commoner in so many ways. Eric wanted her for her mind and beauty and what he would make of her. Jessica had the potential to be ... what? ... Eric's Mona Lisa?

Eric laughed. Jessica was not a weak girl waiting for someone like Eric to change her into what he wanted. They were married for less than three years and like the other wives, she divorced him for incompatibility. She didn't want to be Eric's definition of perfect. At least Jessica didn't take the money and run. She walked away with her pride and confidence intact and that was enough for her. She and Eric continued to like each other.

Eric finished his drink; the fourth double since dinner. He was lonely. He could go to his club and lose some money at poker with his high roller friends. He could go to the Paradise Lounge and buy some drinks for the divorcees in residence and maybe take one of them home. God forbid; not another Doris mistake. He made another Scotch on the rocks and wandered through his penthouse condo. He shook his head as his eye surveyed his possessions and registered 'good taste,' 'affluent,' 'nearly perfect'...

Nearly perfect ... It is very true that money can't make life perfect. Eric returned to his leather recliner and forced himself to take a few breaths and RELAX. He could feel that his damn high blood pressure was way up. The final divorce decree was on the coffee table: signed, sealed and delivered. Another love episode torn asunder. He told himself to be honest about Doris. She was twenty five years his junior and frisky in the sack. There wasn't enough Viagra in the world for him to keep up with her. Besides, Viagra and his high blood pressure medication were as compatible as Doris and himself discussing life. Eric finally dozed off thinking that if he made as many mistakes in business as he did at love, he'd be a Walmart greeter instead of very rich and very lonely.

Eric woke to the living room lights on and his back screaming after sleeping on the recliner for six bloody hours. He extricated himself from the reclining torture and staggered to the bathroom. The pulsating shower massaged enough kinks out of his body to get him upright. He put on a Gucci robe and made a double espresso. He got out his laptop and opened the New York Times for his morning amusement. He scrolled to the financial section and smiled at choosing the lucrative stock option and becoming even wealthier. He moved to the Arts section and on the front page was a photo of Jessica, number one wife. She had written and directed another hit play for Broadway. Eric would send her two dozen muti-colored roses congratulating her on the success. Good old Jessica; she was a self-made work of art.

Eric made another double espresso and sat looking at Jessica on his computer screen. She was still so very beautiful. He opened Google and searched her bio. She was unmarried and seemingly unattached. She'd only been married once, to him, and that was many years ago. Eric wondered if she might be a lesbian or a playgirl that didn't settle with one person: no, that wasn't Jessica. Eric closed his eyes and thought about Jessica and those lovely days they had together. Images of Monet's **Water Lilies** and Van Gogh's **Sunflowers** with Jessica lounging in the background flooded his morning reverie.

Eric was flying first-class to New York on the direct noon flight. He'd telephoned Jessica and asked if she could get him a ticket to her play tonight. She was gracious as always. Eric always made a point of seeing her when he was in the Big Apple. She was probably his only close woman friend. As the plane bounced on turbulent air over Colorado, Eric thought that Jessica was the only lover or wife that he maintained close and honest contact with. Maybe, she was the only lover that wanted to stay in contact with him too. He closed his eyes in first class luxury and had a sweet dream of the college Eric and the virginal Jessica going on their first date to see Joni Mitchell in concert.

Jessica had two box seats reserved for the evening performance. She sat by Eric. He thoroughly enjoyed the show and thought the middle-aged character was repeating some lines he had used thirty years ago. It seemed those lines got the biggest laugh. After the show, Jessica and he went back to her apartment for a drink and to catch up. He looked at her place and the furnishings were like Jessica: simple, elegant, functional, straightforward and perfect.

Jessica yawned. Eric glanced at his Rolex and over two hours had passed. He looked at her and said, "I apologize my dear. I've lost track of the time." He was sitting on the end of the couch looking at her curled up on the far end. He got up and said, "I just enjoy your companionship too much. Thank you so much."

Jessica smiled and walked him to the door. She looked into his dollar green eyes and stammered, "Eric, it's a little late for you to get to your hotel easily. You could sleep on the couch here."

Eric wanted to say yes or thanks but... He stood with the door open and one foot in and one foot out. He was leaving and staying. Jessica took his hand and led him back in. Eric couldn't stop himself; he blurted, "I love you."

Jessica gave him her best Mona Lisa smile.

The Old Man and the Turkeys: A Thanksgiving Story
By Sherry Hunter

The old man lived alone except for his fuzzy cat, Max. He was a tall man, with snowy white hair and he walked with the aid of a tall cane. Max and the tall old man lived in a little house, in a quiet village by a beautiful blue lake. He had friendly neighbors, and there were always pleasant things to do. However, the old man and his fuzzy cat Max did not like to do any of those pleasant things. They did not like their friendly neighbors. The old man was crabby and grumpy and so was Max. He did not have friends. He did not care!

One day, he decided that he wanted to live in a fancy house on the top of a hill where they could look down on their neighbors and snoop. The old man stomped his cane, and decided to go look for a fancy house on a hill. He put Max into his car, and off they went.

They drove to the top of a tall hill in a nearby city, and there among the magnificent houses was the perfect house. It looked down on the other houses and they could see in the windows in order to snoop. Their own house was mysterious, with tall trees and bushes growing all around, so no one could look in and snoop on them.

Soon after they moved into their grand house, they noticed that many wild deer and turkeys were in the streets and yards, wandering aimlessly about. That was interesting!

There was a loud knock on the door. A bunch of important looking people were standing on their porch. "We are the Neighborhood Association representatives," they said. "We decide all of the important things that happen in this neighborhood! You and Max just can't do anything you want to do here. You cannot scare the deer or wild turkeys and you cannot make them unhappy. The deer and wild turkeys lived here first. They are allowed to do anything or eat anything they want. They may eat your flowers and bushes. You are not allowed to put up fences to keep them out. If the deer or turkeys are in the road, you are to stay out of their way! You cannot drive if they are on the road."

Max thought that was all pretty silly, and the tall grumpy old man hated for anyone to tell him what to do, so he loudly stomped his tall cane, and said "Humpf."

All summer Max and the old man sat out on their deck and looked down on the neighbors... snooping. They watched busy families and children working and playing, laughing and crying. They watched the neighbors fix up their houses and they watched the deer eat all the flowers and bushes. They saw the turkeys scratch up the grass and mess up the walks and decks.

They laughed when the turkeys flew up into the trees and perched on branches, or roofs of houses, waiting to fly down at the people when they came out their doors. The people would scream and run, but then the Neighborhood Association representatives would get mad at the people for scaring the turkeys.

They watched people trying to drive their cars on streets covered with turkeys and lined with deer. The cars would run into each other to avoid hitting the animals. By now the deer had more babies and so did the turkeys, and they invited other turkeys and deer to join them too. Since the people protected the deer and turkeys, they did not have to look for food or shelter and they got fat and lazy. Before long, they had eaten all the bushes, flowers and grass and had nothing more to eat, but they didn't stop having more babies, or inviting other deer and turkeys to move in, too.

Soon, there were not enough branches on the trees for the turkeys to perch, so they perched across the roofs of all the houses where their sharp claws made holes in the roofs. When it rained, the roofs started to leak and there were slippery turkey feathers everywhere. People were falling down in heaps.

The neighbors were afraid to come out, because the hungry turkeys would fly at them and take away whatever they had in their hands and fly back to their perch with it and eat it up.

It was almost Thanksgiving and the people in all the houses remembered the pioneers and the first Thanksgiving celebration. They decided it would be good to hunt the wild turkeys and eat them like in the pioneer days.

"We have been feeding them all summer with our bushes, flowers, grass and the things they steal out of our hands," the neighbors said. "Now we will eat them; it is only fair.

"No. No, No! Absolutely not!" said the important Neighborhood Association representatives. "The turkeys and deer can go anywhere, eat what they want, and do anything they want to do!"

The deer and turkeys got bolder! One day a deer chased a little girl into her house from the school bus. The turkeys would fly down and land on people's heads and make them carry them about. The deer and turkeys became naughty, hateful bullies, but the grumpy old man and Max just snooped and laughed

One day, the old man and Max noticed a little boy and his sister looking out their window at all the turkeys and deer. They were crying because they were afraid to go outside to play. Max laughed at the sad little boy and girl and the grumpy old man stomped his cane in glee. Then they saw two older boys who were playing catch with their baseball, but some hungry turkeys flew at the ball, grabbed it and ate it up. The boys watched the turkeys in disbelief. Max laughed until he fell over. Plop! and the old man stomped his cane in delight.

All the turkeys and deer gave the the old man and Max dirty looks and growled at them. The turkeys and deer did not like to be laughed at by the human and cat bullies, even though they were bullies themselves.

"Let's go to the donut shop," the old man said to Max. "We will celebrate all the fun we are having."

Max smiled a huge cat smile. He loved donuts. He ran to get in the car. The old man started to back his car out of the garage, but he slammed on his brakes in shock. His driveway was full of turkeys; the street was covered with them; there were turkeys as far as the eye could see. The turkeys ran into his garage. He could not back his car out without hitting a turkey. They couldn't get out of their car... The moment they started to open the door to get out, the turkeys would fly in. The old man started honking the horn, hoping the turkeys would go away and that someone would hear and come help them. In frustration, the old man stomped his cane. The turkeys were not so funny to the old man and his cat now!

Suddenly, there was a loud roaring sound coming from the nearby street. They looked out the car window and saw a large group of Neighborhood Association representatives coming into view. They had leaf-blowing machines and they were pointing them at the turkeys, blowing them aside so they could make a path. They blew turkeys to the left; they blew turkeys to the right. They blew turkeys up into the air and had them tumbling everywhere. Finally, the old man and Max were able to get out of the car and join the others in the garage.

The old man, the cat and the representatives all worked their way through the confused turkeys to the door of the house, but before they could get in, the turkeys flew at them, knocked them over and got into the house first. Max let out a loud frightened wail.

Once the turkeys were inside, they flew at the door and slammed it shut. They locked it so the people and the cat could not get in. The grumpy old man stomped his cane, but it did not make the situation better. The turkeys had taken over his house!

"I don't understand you mean turkeys," he shouted angrily at them. "I was on your side, rooting for you when you picked on all the people, especially the children." The turkeys just laughed, because that is what bully turkeys do!

All of the representatives with the leaf blowers were gathered in a huddle. "What are we going to do now?" they lamented. "This was the last house to save from the turkeys. They have taken control of every house in the neighborhood and won't let anyone in!"

The people were gathered around outside. They were all cold and hungry and the grumpy old man and Max were cold and hungry, too.

The people decided to build a bonfire in the old man's backyard, because his house was the highest on the hill, and they could look down and snoop on the turkeys and make decisions. The turkeys had taken over everything – even the deer. They were telling the deer to go away to another neighborhood.

The turkeys were eating food out of the cupboards and refrigerators and sleeping in the people's beds. They were wearing the children's clothes and brushing their beaks with the children's toothbrushes. They were playing with the children's toys and watching their televisions. Some turkeys were gathered around tables eating and playing cards. They had fires in the fireplaces and were cozy and warm. The turkeys were not hungry anymore, but the people were. The turkeys were inside the houses and the people were locked outside.

The people knocked on the doors of their houses. They looked in the windows, but the turkeys gave them dirty looks and laughed at them. The people gathered around the bonfire. They were hungry. The children were crying. They wanted their dinner, their nice warm beds and they wanted to play with their games and read their books. The adults were sad because they could not do anything to get their houses back. It was almost Thanksgiving and there would be no turkey dinner... the turkeys would be eating the people's dinner instead.

The grumpy old man stomped his tall cane and then angrily stomped it again, but to no avail!

Max the cat was not laughing at others anymore. Now Max and the old man knew what it was like to be bullied. It hurt! It was not funny when you were the victim!

Max curled up in a little girl's lap and purred softly when she stroked his head. He stopped shivering. He felt warm all over, and thought this was the nicest little girl he ever knew. For the first time in his life Max understood what it meant to be loved and needed by someone.

The next morning when everyone awoke, the bonfire was out and it was raining.

"What are we going to do?" they all wondered. Then they saw a large flock of turkeys approaching them. The turkeys looked important and very official. They even wore badges that said "Turkey Representative." The turkeys had bows and arrows and a large piece of official looking paper. A big Tom Turkey handed the paper to one of the important representative people.

"This is your official notice!" the Tom Turkey said loudly. "You must leave your houses and the neighborhood immediately! It is ours now! We have taken it back, so just go away!"

Max mewed sadly and the old man stomped his tall cane with a loud hard thud! He knew in his heart that cane stomping did no good, but he loudly stomped it anyway. He was hungry and he was cold!...

The old man woke up with a start! "Where am I?" he wondered. "Oh my! I am having a very bad dream!" His covers were kicked off his bed onto the floor. He was cold. His tummy growled; he was hungry. He could hear Max purring, but he could not see the fuzzy fat cat.

He opened his eyes and sat up in bed. The dream seemed so real, but here he was in his own bed, in his own little house, in the quiet village by the beautiful blue lake. He could hear the clatter of pans coming from the kitchen, and could hear his sweet little old wife singing a cheerful song as she prepared the turkey for dinner that day. The old man sighed in relief.

Max was curled up at the foot of the bed sleeping peacefully. Then he remembered that today was Thanksgiving and his children, grandchildren and friends were coming for dinner. There were lots of chores to be done to get everything ready. He must get up and help his wife prepare for the day.

The old man stood up, yawned and stretched his tall body up even taller. "I am glad it is Thanksgiving today," he said to Max. "I am thankful that you are my cat. I am thankful for my pretty little house, for my pleasant little village, the beautiful blue lake and all the fun and interesting things there are to do here. I am thankful for my happy old wife, for my children and my beautiful grandchildren. I am thankful for my food and my healthy body. I am thankful for my friends too. I am so thankful that today is Thanksgiving Day, and all day long I can be thankful. I am going to tell everyone how thankful I am.

Max purred contentedly. He was thankful, too. He did not like that grand big house in the city and he did not like living with all those turkeys!

Sky Pond & The Friendship Leaves

A story for all ages
By Bridgett Johnson-Elliott

There once was a small, forgotten pond that resided at the end of an old street. Sky Pond was the water's name, and she was very lonely. Sky Pond sat alone day after day, season after season, her only company the raindrops and the reflection of the changing sky drifting across her waters. Sky Pond was formed many years ago from the hollowed out space left by a fallen tree, long before the street was built and the people moved in. Sky Pond enjoyed many a precipitous winters but always stayed small and contained within her circular tree hollow.

Sky Pond had many visitors. Sometimes from jumping toddlers with muddy alligator boots and high-pitched squeals. Often, young people who stood right over Sky Pond and laughed at their reflections.

Clara, the little girl who lived across the street, came to visit Sky Pond's waters. She arrived in fresh, clean clothes with a head full of blond curls. She left with clumps of grass dreadlocks and mud on every inch of skin. Sky Pond wondered if all children liked to get dirty like this. Clara spoke in great detail about the legends of mythical sea creatures and enchanted mermaids. Sky Pond didn't have anything interesting like that in her waters, except for some boring mud snails and periwinkles.

Sky Pond was visited by Harley, a stocky pug who went on daily walks with his owners. Harley wore a miniature leather jacket bearing his name in orange letters, with the emblem of a pug riding a motorcycle. Harley became thirsty on his walks, and helped himself to slobbering drinks of Sky Pond's water. He, of course, drank too fast and sneezed water snot all over Sky Pond. It was hard not to laugh at his terrible manners. Sky Pond would have scolded him, but she didn't think Harley would listen to her.

Sky Pond was visited by a quiet grey cat named Echo. Echo was polite and courteous with lovely eyes the color of jade. Her tiny pink tongue made soft ripples in the water as she drank. Echo always nodded a silent "thank you" before she pranced away. Sky Pond would have replied, but she thought Echo, a highly intelligent feline, would think it beneath her to converse with a pond.

In the springtime, the frogs lived with Sky Pond, much to her dislike. They croaked all night long, jumping and hopping around in her waters, trying to attract a mate. They were such showoffs! She couldn't get a wink of sleep with all those off-key croaks and love-sick "ribbits."

Sky Pond longed for a friend of her own. A cheerful friend who wouldn't splash around or muddy her waters, and would like her just the way she was, even if she wasn't a fancy pond with lily pads and koi fish.

Sometimes, when you can't find a friend, you have to wait for one to find you.

Sky Pond waited. And waited. She passed season after season this way. In her lonely boredom, she ignored all the life passing by her street. Sky Pond spent her time counting mud skippers in her waters, and watching bird droppings hit the sidewalk. She barely even noticed when a passerby accidentally dropped their ham and cheese sandwich in her waters. It had floated there all day before a crow took pity and scooped it out.

Sky Pond could hear her own loneliness every time the rain fell. Plop! Plop! Plop! Such a sad sound.

Then, one magic autumn day, something happened. Sky Pond met a friend! It came when she least expected it, and in a most graceful way. A single yellow maple leaf was tossed from a tree across the street and floated down into her waters. The kindly Breeze, knowing of Sky Pond's loneliness, had sent the leaf in her direction.

Goldie was the maple leaf's name. Goldie had spent the whole summer in the branches of the old maple tree, dancing with her brothers and sisters, telling stories together and laughing with the summer wind. They had watched everything from up above, and saw Sky Pond's sadness. Goldie said she had been waiting for the right time to come visit Sky Pond.

"The maple leaves remain on the trees until nights become colder and days have less light," Goldie explained. "Once our beautiful green coat changes to yellow and amber, we are finally able to let go of the branches and cascade down to earth!" "We saw you, Sky Pond, and wished that you were not so sad. It turns your waters into an inky black shadow where no light gets in." "If only you would look up and see us waving at you!"

Sky Pond listened to all this with a reflective stillness befitting water. "I didn't know," Sky Pond replied in a tender voice. "I stopped noticing things around me because I thought no one cared." "I was so in need of a friend."

Goldie gave Sky Pond a beaming, crinkled leaf-smile, and said, "You always have a friend in me." "In fact, Sky Pond, you have not just one, but dozens and dozens of friends!" All my sisters and brothers want to come meet you. The kindly Breeze will send them over to your waters, and we will celebrate together!"

Soon, many more maple leaves came to join Sky Pond and Goldie. They talked, laughed and told stories. A rich friendship was born, turning the water into a garden of autumnal colors. People came to watch Sky Pond, Goldie and the leaves. They forgot where they were. The old pond at the end of the pot-holed street was transformed into a place of magic and beauty.

It was soon after that Clara came to visit on her bike. Sky Pond had not seen Clara for many seasons. Her family had moved to a smaller house a few miles away. Clara looked older from the last time Sky Pond had seen her. Her legs and arms were longer. Her curly blond hair had lost most its curl and become darker. Today, Clara did not head for the mud. She spread a blanket out by Sky Pond and sat down with a book. Then, after a contented hour had passed, Clara set her book down and pulled a small, gold mirror out of her pocket. Clara had read that if you watched the reflection of water through a mirror, it might reveal your future.

The moment Clara turned the mirror toward the water, Sky Pond could see her own reflection for the very first time. She could see Goldie and all the leaves surrounding her like a multi-colored blanket. She could see how the sun shone bright across a bluebird autumn sky and clouds drifted by like ships at sea. She could see green pebbles in the bottom of her clear waters. It was a beautiful sight. Sky Pond filled herself up with tears of happiness that she was no longer alone. She realized that she had never been alone. All of nature and life surrounded her.

When the next jumping toddler came by, Sky Pond would help them to make big, happy splashes in her waters. When a passerby stopped to laugh at their reflection, Sky Pond would laugh with them!

The next time Sky Pond saw the pug, Harley, she'd instruct him to sip water, not gulp, and that no matter how excited he became, he should never sneeze on anyone.

When Echo arrived on her little cat feet, Sky Pond would enjoy the quiet they shared together, sitting side by side in perfect stillness. She realized that they could communicate everything by saying nothing. It might look like napping, but it was the practice of perfect Zen.

The coming spring when the frogs emerged, Sky Pond would listen to them sing. She would look up at the night sky and discover how their music made the stars dance, the moon wink and the earth come alive again.

Sky Pond would always be grateful to Clara for showing her the reflection of true friendship. It would stay with her always. Sky Pond had seen Clara's future in the mirror's reflection, and knew it'd be filled with bright, exciting adventures ahead. Clara would come back again with many new stories to tell Sky Pond.

These thoughts gave Sky Pond confidence for the coming winter, when her pond froze over and the street became cold and still. Sky Pond knew Goldie and all her leaf friends would be gone. However, she wouldn't be sad. Sky Pond knew Goldie's spirit would return as a fresh new leaf, and the following autumn they would reunite. They'd celebrate with all the leaves at having come full circle again through the changing seasons.

"A little friendship goes a long way," thought Sky Pond. She looked up with a contented smile as the last rays of sunset shone gold upon her waters.

Just One Billy Goat Gruff
By Muriel Linder

To an outsider, it would seem that my Dad has a firm handle on most everything. Don't get me wrong. He isn't a dictator. But my brother and I have learned the importance of consulting him before going ahead with our plans. He takes pride in being the head of his household. Anyway, Mom is smart enough to go along with this arrangement and let him think so. She has a coy way of planting an idea in Dad's head, and then watching it take root and become his own.

Dad is a big, barrel-chested, clean shaven redneck, who turns into a marshmallow at the sight of tears. We kids have learned to work this to our advantage. And work it we have, except for one time when the billy goat came to dinner.

Bobby, my little brother, is known at school as a push-over for bringing all the undesirable, dysfunctional pets of the neighborhood home. After school, Mom would watch for Bobby coming up the sidewalk toward home. Every now and then he'd stop and wait. Soon Mom would see a scraggly fur-ball trailing along behind.

Dad's eyes always misted up and got real shiny when he saw the wretched looking thing, and he and Mom would set about patiently rehabilitating this less fortunate of God's creatures. Usually, they were able to find them homes. Then one evening, Bobby totally overshot his boundaries. He led a full grown billy goat, with eight-inch horns sprouting out the top of his head, into the kitchen.

Mom screamed and turned a molded Jello upside down into a pan of chicken gravy. With his hand pointing toward the back door, Dad said one word. "Out!" Then he stuck his lower lip out and refused to negotiate any kind of a deal with Bobby.

"But the Parkers were going to take him to the place where they make dog food," Bobby wailed.

Dad stood firm. "Take him back." Again, he pointed to the door.

After she rescued the Jello from the gravy, Mom went to look for Bobby. She found him sitting in the driveway on an overturned bucket. He was still hanging onto the goat. For once, Mom overruled Dad and told Bobby he could tie the goat in the corner of the backyard. "But you've got to find a home for him before dark," she said.

About an hour later, a likely prospect came to visit.

It was Mr. Sherman. He was a bachelor and lived about a mile away on a side road. Next to his house and lot, Mr. Sherman owned an acre of undeveloped property; a tangle of vetch, wild oats, and berry vines. It was a thorn of contention to the neighbors and the city council, but a perfect environment for the goat.

With a firm grip on one horn and the lead rope in the opposite hand, Mr. Sherman set out for home. Dad finally broke his silence and suggested that Bobby go along, "...just in case there is trouble along the way." And trouble there was!

That goat could spot a purple pansy half a block away, and there wasn't a yellow rose left anywhere along the mile route. Several people came out and threatened a surgical procedure right on the spot. This caused Bobby to ask Mom and Dad a lot of questions when he came home. Frankly, I couldn't figure out the connection between the goat's sexuality and his choice of menu.

That night, we laughed about the antics of the goat, and relaxed in the certainty that we had seen the last of him.... But the goat came back!

The next morning Dad found him pruning the neighbors hedge in a most unconventional manner while dragging 30-feet of chain behind him. Dad got Bobby and I out of bed and told us to "Get that damn goat back to Mr. Sherman before the neighbors woke up." One look at Dad's face convinced us to do just as we were told.

Two weeks went by with no sign of the goat. One Sunday afternoon, Mom and Dad went to the nursery to get some bedding plants and a shade tree for the south side of the house. Bobby and I stayed home. We were in the kitchen making sandwiches when... the goat came back!

He walked right through the screen door, let out a bleat, and grabbed my sandwich. Just then Mom and Dad pulled in the driveway. We stared at the goat and then at the huge hole in the screen door. Bobby ran and opened the screen and stood in front of the hole while I attempted to tackle the goat and get him outside, but the goat made a circle around the dining room table and headed upstairs. I cornered him in the bathroom and shut the door. Then I raced back down to Bobby. He was still standing in front of the screen door.

"Where's the goat?" Bobby asked. "In the upstairs bathroom."

"What are we going to do?"

"I'm going to tie some sheets around him and lower him off the balcony. I want you to hang onto the goat when he comes down. First, I gotta call Dave to come and help me get him over the balcony railing."

"What are we going to do with the screen door?" Bobby asked. I walked over and ripped the screen completely out of the door and stuffed it in the bottom of the kitchen garbage bin.

"Leave it open," I told Bobby. "Maybe, they won't notice." Dave arrived and we told him the plan, but before we could carry out our mission, the goat went berserk. There was a terrible crash and the sound of splintering glass, followed by a rattling that literally shook the house.

Mom and Dad came running in the backdoor. They looked from me to Bobby and back at me again.

"What's going on?" Dad bellowed.

"The goat," Bobby whispered.

"Where is it?" Dad hissed.

Just then that loud rattling noise sounded again, and I pointed to the stairs. Dad took the steps two at a time. Dave and I and Bobby were right behind him. "You're right," Bobby whispered. "They didn't even notice the screen door."

When Dad opened the bathroom door, the goat was standing on his hind feet with his front feet in the sink and his horns firmly embedded in the mirrored door of the medicine cabinet.

Dad didn't even swear. He just stood there looking at the goat. Finally, he said, "I don't believe it." He jerked the goat's horns loose, and Dave and I grabbed a horn on each side and hustled the goat down the stairs and out the back door. We never stopped until we got to Mr. Sherman's place.

By the time we got back home, Dad had cleaned up the mess in the bathroom and gone to get another medicine cabinet. The missing screen wasn't discovered until Mom went to shut the door that evening.

For the next two days, every now and then, Dad would shake his head and say "I don't believe it!" When he finally found his voice, Dad promised Bobby and I, "If that goat shows up again, I will personally take him to the dog food plant just like Mr. Parker intended."

Bobby and I kept a very low profile. We did our chores without being told, and didn't ask for a thing. A month went by and slowly everyone began to relax. It was warm summer now, and Bobby and I decided to camp out in the backyard. We pounded some stakes in the ground and draped a tarp over them to keep the dew off our sleeping bags.

Sometime in the night, I felt Bobby breathing down the back of my neck. I nudged him to move over. Next thing I knew, the tarp fell down on us. I woke with a jerk and sat up. I could see the outline of an animal. Yes, the goat had come back! He was eating the corner of our tarp.

I shook Bobby awake. "The goat is back!" I whispered.

We gotta get him outta here before Dad gets up.

Bobby was on his feet in a flash. We put our shoes on and took off in our pajamas with the goat. It was still dark, but by the time we got back from Mr. Sherman's it was getting daylight. We managed to get the tarp back on the stakes, and get in our sleeping bags before Dad came out the backdoor.

Three months went by and we never saw the goat. One day, Bobby asked me to go with him to see Mr. Sherman. "I hope he didn't take Billy Goat to the dog food place," Bobby said.

When we got there, Mr. Sherman was having lunch, and there in the kitchen was Billy Goat standing by the table eating out of a plate.

"He just wanted a little human companionship," Mr. Sherman said.

A Walk in the Forest
Turas: Spiraling Walk Prayer/Journey
By Liath MacTire

I came to a three-pronged fork in the forest road on my second morning in the woods. Two of the roads were pretty clear: cut and graveled for timber hauling by a logging company. Those roads were almost sure to lead to recent clear cuts, and I wasn't in the mood to spend time admiring stumps and stacks of limbs waiting for controlled burns. Then there was the third road, more of an almost hidden path. I thought this hidden path was not the sort of road a neophyte forest walker would take, unless they were looking to find something more than a tree-lined gravel road. I took it. Friendly sort of trail really. Overgrown with tree branches and bushes reaching out from each side to block my passage. Yet I had no difficulty finding my way. The ground showed evidence of traffic. Wild and ferocious beasts often passed this way, no doubt.

The ferocious beast currently in residence is a blue-throated lizard sunning on a rock. He and I pass the time of day, sharing the warmth of the morning sun with frequent head bobs.

The path led around the side of the mountain, through the forest, and with many ups and just as many downs. There were a lot of arounds, overs, unders, too, but it never did steer consistently in any one direction. Just right of the path, up the side of the mountain, were occasional bare patches of earth that held deep imprints from the passing who left the path to strike out for greener pastures, for home or whatever took their fancy further up the mountain. Once, late in the afternoon, I came upon a positive feast of tracks. At least four or five deer, what looked to be a family of raccoons with three or four kits, and finally, partially overlaying a rock, but still showing in the mud, was the track of a hunter – large dog, bear, cougar, I couldn't tell. The track was too indistinct, and I am not a skilled tracker. Just a forest wanderer with a camera. As far as I could tell, there were no other similar tracks nearby, so the hunter got to keep its secrets, but I took a few photos from different angles so perhaps I could identify my hunter later – sort of benevolent armchair hunt of hunters.

My path wandered on, crossing gullies, climbing hillocks, and almost disappeared in an occasional patch of very dense forest underbrush. These are not the open-floored forests of the south. Forests here are filled with ferns and bushes and vines. In some areas, I have even found a charming fellow named the Devil's Club. If you should come upon a Devil threatening you with one of these clubs I advise you to go somewhere else. Quickly.

Find a photo of a Devil's Club, if you can. Get to know that club. That Devil is not your friend, but the Club just might be. I understand from an herb lady friend that the Devil's Club has a bunch of beneficial medicinal uses.

This path is an odd path. By now, I've been walking, and I must admit gawking for hours and yet it has not faded or become smaller or larger. It just continues in much the same manner it started, heavily lined with brush and branches and the now and then invitation to wander off to one side or the other. When I first stepped onto the path, much of the surrounding forest looked like it had been logged fifty or sixty years ago. The forest around me now is older – Old Growth for certain. Many of the trees looked ancient. If I were walking in a fantasy story, I would expect some of these trees to open eyes and inspect me. Alas, they remain asleep ignoring my passage. When I take their photo, they don't seem to mind at all.

The time has come to set up camp. I am one of those finicky campers. I insist upon all of the niceties of modern camping: tent, bedroll, fire ring, a branch to hang my pack out of the reach of nocturnal visitors. I travel in style. This night, there is an almost full moon, a cold moon. Low, thin clouds speed across the face of the moon as though they had somewhere important they just had to be. The temperature drops quickly. I am alone with my notebook, sitting cross-legged by my fire, watching all the eyes watching me from the surrounding woods. That's one of the nice things about camping alone. With a chattering group of fellow campers swapping hoary stories and singing bawdy songs, the eyes never appear. Sometimes, I think the eyes are all my imagination, and sometimes, I think the eyes are there when I have my friends with me, but I'm too distracted to notice. Doesn't much matter. I like to think the eyes are there and always will be.

Daylight comes and I don't wanna go home. I like the feel here, and my wandering path beckons with an almost palpable pull. I remember the eyes last night and decide to stroll to the edge of camp, camera in hand, to look for tracks of what might have been watching me. I find tracks. Coyote tracks run crazy trails in all directions through my camp – Coyote by the score. Mister Coyote brought the family for a middle-of-the-night party. I consider myself a light sleeper in the wild. I am kidding myself. During the night, a fog has dampened every exposed surface – every exposed surface except for the two smooth, dry spots, one on each side of my bedroll. During the night I had shared my bed space with a couple of coyotes looking for a three-dog night. They had lain with me for a warm snuggle, I suppose, and left with not so much as a fair-thee-well. Such fickleness, and after all I did for them. No doubt, they had a fine time laughing at my dullness. Coyotes always have, and always will have, the upper paw. We may have created civilization for our own purposes but, Coyote has put our civilization to his own use.

I spend considerable thought and time on the preparation of my breakfast. I am told by those with great authority on the subject, that breakfast is the most important meal of the day. Today my path might be more demanding than yesterday, so best to be prepared. Two energy bars and a pot of Devil's Club Tea, brewed up in cowboy-coffee style, and I am ready to hiker up. I am off to test my mettle with the wildness of my magical path. What makes this path magical? An aura, a feeling, a light surrounding the ferns, towering cedars and hemlocks. Something almost tangible has created a sense of magic and wonder, and I feel I am becoming part of it. This path is green – very green indeed. I'm not an artist, except of course for the doodling. If I were ever to take up paints, I would have my green period. There are so many incarnations of the color green.

There are places in a forest that are passive; and other places are active. My path is active. Sometimes people can sense when they are being watched. On my path, there is a tangible feel of eyes watching me. Perhaps judging me for potential as a danger or perhaps my watchers are simply curious. I can hear movement of small and hidden beasties. That is unusual. I guess my hearing is as good as most, but I don't often hear the small ones in the brush and trees. I can't see or hear any sign of a river, but I know there must be water somewhere near. I can smell the water, there are dragonflies scooting back and forth. They wouldn't be here without water. A really stunning dragonfly dressed in greens and blues and golds with a hint of red comes to me and stares intently into my face. I bring my camera up to focus on my dragonfly, and she moves back a couple of feet to hang motionless in the air examining me. The perfect subject in the perfect pose; the perfect photo.

My wee dragon suddenly whirls about and quite emphatically suggests that if I'm coming to visit I'd better put some bustle in my get-a-long. Her words, not mine. Dragon's home is a pond she shares with the dragonfly community. Brilliant colors are everywhere, streaking, hovering, darting. This community is busy doing whatever it is dragonflies do in morning sunlight. Mostly, they flit about with extraordinary energy, while discussing the most amazing deeds and events of days long past. I am not much for flitting about, and I am not well informed on the past glories of dragonflies. I believe my best option is to sit a spell and listen to stories of great deeds. A nice cuppa Devil's Club tea would go well at this point.

Do you suppose the biggest, baddest dragonfly once whipped the snot out of a really big lizard? Do you suppose leg-pulling is the happy pastime at the Dragonfly condominium? The morning passes with the dragonflies engaging in a energetic leg-pulling contest. I supplied the legs. I finish my tea and make my way back to my path.

I am not really hiking my path. More of a stroll going up and down and around. The green of the ferns and underbrush becomes more intense in some places and fades in others. Once again, I have the sense of being watched, but I see no beastie about. Although it's been over an hour since I left the dragonflies, the path has taken so many turns and detours that I am probably not more than a couple of thousand yards from the dragonflies.

Normally I am sharp-eyed when I'm running around in the forest. You really have to be aware of what might be around you. Very few hikers want to take a turn around a boulder and pass the time of day with a black bear or cougar. The outcome of those meetings is not always happy for the hiker and sometimes not so happy for the bear or cougar. The meetings are in doubt at best. Today there are no bears, no cougars, not even a lonely coyote. My watcher is somewhere about and at last I spot her. She is perched on a branch ten feet away and fifteen feet up. Who you might ask is this watcher? The *"whoo"* is appropriate. A great owl stares at me with an intensity that could be matched only by another owl. I'm not an owl and I don't accept the stare-down contest. Instead I wish the owl a good morning and continue on my mysterious magical path.

I stop, however, when Owl does a fair impression of the Cheshire Cat. Not the smile, but rather the ability to speak English. No simple whoo or hoot for this owl. No, this Owl wishes me "a pleasant walk" and suggests I "might want to find shelter before the storm." The whole business is ridiculous. There's no sign of a storm. Not even a breeze. And why would I need to find shelter? I mean, really, I should hide from a bit of rain? I say as much to the Owl and Owl responds with, "A thing is right when it tends to preserve the integrity, stability, and beauty of the biotic community. It is wrong when it tends otherwise." First Owl tells me to find shelter and now Owl is quoting Aldo Leopold to me. I find this a bit odd. Yet I have no sense that Owl is picking up where the Dragonflies left off with the leg pulling. I fail to understand how coming in from the rain relate to Aldo's Axiom.

"So tell me Owl, what is right and what is not right with this forest?" No reply from Owl except for two short side hops along her branch and a conspiratorial blink. Could there be meaning in taking two hops and a blink? A secret language? A code? What is Owl telling me? If we don't stop doing the "not right" things the forest is doomed and by extension, humanity along with it? Or perhaps Owl is telling me the biosphere is filled with life and all that life is interconnected and interdependent. One enormous multiheaded symbiosis... me, the dragonflies, the coyotes, Owl – all cousins? I could fix you up with my cousin the squid. Friendly sort of fellow, you'd like him. Maybe Owl is telling me I've been hitting the Devil's

Club tea a little too hard, and there is such a thing as unintended consequences. My conversation with Owl is no doubt one of those consequences that were unintended.

Perhaps I am being dense and do not understand the subtleties of Owl's mind. Owl blinks and if an owl could smile, I swear this owl is smiling. I have the impression that Owl is about to say something like, "Continue your path of mystery, Grasshopper." I wish Owl a fine day and set off when Owl shudders, chirps, and brings up a packet of mousie bones. The packet drops at my feet. "A present. For me? You shouldn't have." Owl hoots, blinks, and falls asleep.

The sun is overhead, but not penetrating to the forest floor. The canopy filters out direct sunlight giving my path that deep-green subdued look. I work my camera overtime. Ferns, vines, an occasional tree, holes in the ground hiding the mysterious underground citizens lying in wait for a time to come out and go shopping for dinner. I am having more fun than I've had in years. I could, if I was of a mind, drop out of school, take up the mantle of Ansel Adams, and live my life as a wilderness photographer. My magical path could provide me with the inspiration that Yosemite provided for. All I lack is his talent, creativity, and dedication to his art.

The thought occurs to me that this path I am walking is one of the odder paths I've walked during a life full of paths. But then, it may be just my imagination. Imagination or not, this mystery path shows no sign of ending. I need a campsite for the night. I round a bend and there, in much splendor and glory is a meadow wetland. The high forest canopy that has filtered the sun is pushed back and now surrounds the meadow in a great circle. Everything is right with the world.

The sun, the birds, and the chirping of a highly motivated and persistent squirrel have come together to fill me with an almost cozy feeling. The grass in the meadow is knee high and a light breeze disturbs the stalks just the right amount. The grass waves hello and I wave back and take my first step into the meadow. Of course, I should have known. If I had thought for just a moment everything would have become clear instead of wet. A meadow like this, in the middle of a forest is, by all rights home to a beaver. Maybe a whole beaver clan. Beavers build things: dams, lodges, meadows, and in the end, they create wetlands. And that is what I have here. I step off the path, cross a downed, decaying log and walk into the sea of grass. No, that's not quite right. I walk through the grass and into calf-deep pond water. Somewhere close a beaver tail slaps the water. Walking in wet boots is not much fun, so now is the perfect time for me, my boots, and my socks to bask on a log to dry in the sun. Time to head for home but first another cuppa tea is in order.

Something for Jimmy
By Jeanette-Marie Mirich

With a hand above her eyes, Linda Frazier shaded the glare of the setting sun. She stared hard over the golden water toward a boy floating on an inner tube. Aubergine clouds plumed the horizon. Toes imbedded in the crunchy sand of the seashore, Linda stood rigidly still. The tension in her shoulders had been with her all day. Keeping her eyes fixed on her small son, Linda waggled her head back and forth over her shoulders, trying to ease the ache that had settled like a firebrand. *Comes from living in the midst of noise*, she decided, unhappy with her third floor apartment near the railroad tracks. As evening shadows caressed the dunes she decided it was time to leave.

Linda knew her blue polka-dot sundress was out of place among the sunbathers. Hadn't she been reminded earlier when watching Jimmy hop down the stairs as she exited the apartment? That was before Mrs. De-Maio had slammed open her door at the noise of his shoes, then scanned them with squinty eyes. Linda had grabbed Jimmy's small hand.

"Looking high and mighty for a beach picnic," the woman had stated, sneering at Linda's navy espadrilles. Taking a long drag on her cigarette, her neighbor let the smoke fill the space between them. "Going to have tea with the Queen?"

Linda had laughed softly so Jimmy wouldn't be alarmed at the tension. She waved her newly-polished nails as a greeting, then let her hand drop. The shiny red nails against her blue and white dress reminded her of a flag with drops of blood cascading across the field of stars.

Her son was not alone. Linda never let him go anywhere without a guardian. The sheltered spit of land facing the Virginia naval yards had been Mike's hometown, not hers. After a year she was still learning street names. Linda narrowed her chocolate brown eyes as her youngest brother paddled alongside the rolling dark ring of rubber.

Ready to grow taller than his five-foot-nine inches, John had awkwardly hunched his shoulders as he carried the basket toward the trolley. That morning, making her promise not to tell their father, he had spoken of enlisting, now that he was seventeen. She hadn't commented, but bent to tie Jimmy's shoelace, not giving John eye contact.

Linda shuddered at the thought of her youngest brother heading off to war, perhaps be assigned to their father's Pacific fleet as a lowly, deck-scrubbing seaman. She frowned as a westerly breeze lifted the tangle of curls that ribboned her shoulders. Again the familiar tension arched along her shoulders.

Her eyes flicked to the shore littered with the remains of a summer day—a small metal pail missing its handle, a deflated ball and a striped towel. At her feet was the wicker basket that had held their sandwiches and a thermos of water. Quickly she stuffed in the wax paper squares, napkins, and thermos, flipping the lid shut with a bang.

There were other swimmers in the water, children splashing in the shallows, a couple lying on a towel, the woman's toes massaging the man's calves. The thought, odd to see a man not in uniform, was pushed aside by the memory of how terrified she had been when Jimmy begged to swim.

He frightened her with his male bravado. Linda chewed her bottom lip and stuffed her panic down. Down past the ruby lips, choking throat, and into the recesses of her stomach. Fear burned there, but she didn't scream. She had saved herself that embarrassment and Jimmy too. Could a six-year-old recover from an hysterical mother?

"You are so like your father," Linda whispered in the rising wind. A tight smile flicked across her lips, then vanished as she remembered her little boy paddling out from the shore without looking back. Just like Mike hadn't looked back either when he'd joined the Army Air Corps, and months later, grinning goodbye, had disappeared onto the belching train that would take him north.

Mike's letters had arrived sporadically, then not at all. On an October raid his plane became an incandescent golden ball over Dresden. Nothing remained of him but memories, a few pictures and a small box with a note from his commanding officer. The box sat on her dresser top. It contained a note, a recitation really, of how brave he had been. "One of my best pilots," he had underlined. The words were stilted, as if Mike's C.O. wrote dozens a day. The postscript at least had been human.

"Something for Jimmy," he had cribbed, tucking in a Purple Heart. Linda had thrown it across the room and screamed. Beside Mike's grandfather's grave was the marker with Mike's date of birth and date of death. Her fingers had brailled his name as a bugler played taps.

Linda brushed away sudden tears, then lifting her straw hat she frantically waved it against the humid air. The boy in green swim trunks waggled his fingers with nonchalance, then dipped a hand over the side of his inflated ring and oared against the current.

He was drifting south. John, legs tucked into the tube, was riding the waves with him. Linda walked along the shore keeping pace. Sand hissed against her bare feet. The sky streaked with sherbet streamers spread across the water, undulating with the waves.

We'll have ice cream for dinner, Linda decided. A swirl of water lapped over her ankles. The bay was warm. She chuckled softly, letting the unfamiliar sound fill her throat and displace the gnawing fear. With her head lifted toward the offshore breeze that ruffled the Chesapeake water, she expelled a breath as if she were blowing smoke rings. Jimmy was rocking contentedly on the soft rolling waves. Linda listened to the palm fronds gentle clack, then shook her head as if clearing it. She hiked up to dry sand where a tuff of seagrass sashayed in the breeze. Tossing her hat and shoes beside it she unbuttoned her dress. When the cloth pooled around her feet she picked it up with her toes and kicked the swirl of colors toward the rest of her things. She softly smiled, because her swimsuit matched her dress and, if she had known, her neighbor would remark caustically about her frivolity.

Without looking back Linda stepped into the waves and swam lazily toward her son. The boy's eyes stared with surprise. She circled him, pulling his tube behind her.

"Something for Jimmy," Linda murmured, letting laughter fill the air.

Photo Gallery

Vaughn, Oregon (near Crow) was represented in a parade; ca 1920.
Photo from the Clair and Iola Stephens' collection

Dr. Sparky
By Mario

My name is Ezra Watson. I live here in Eugene Oregon with my dog Sparky and our only vice is hunting and fishing.

Sparky is a short-haired dog about the size of a Labrador retriever and a good dog to have on the farm. He leaves the chickens and other livestock alone. His only chore is to herd Geraldine home for milking.

If there was one thing Sparky loves, it is fishing. We go to a lake every time work slacked off a bit and camp out. Sparky loves sleeping outside, but hates tents, so I bought a 22-foot camping trailer for him to sleep under. His favorite sleeping quarters were just behind the rear axle.

Old Sparky must have a little Airedale blood in him, for he has a black saddle with brown and white legs and sides. Like all terriers, he is territorial and protective of our space and living quarters.

As soon as he catches a glimpse of my fishing pole, he comes running, as usual. His tongue hangs out and while jumping and frolicking around, he slings saliva and slobbers everywhere. Sparky has one thing in common with me – that dog and I love to fish.

When Sparky reached 1½ years old, I took him aside and said, "Sparky my boy, it's time you got some learnin."

I kenneled him and hustled him off to my brother Lehman for obedience training. Lehman is a professional dog trainer, so I sent $150 along with a return ticket from Texas. Hey, it sure was lonely without my buddy; I called and asked about him every day.

Finally, the day arrived when I was to meet the train and pick him up. Boy was he glad to see me and on his collar was a note from Lehman.

"Ezra, this was the easiest training sessions I've ever experienced. Hated to send this dog back and I'm refunding $50. If you ever want to sell him, I'll give you $500..."

Later in the evening, I sat down and penned a letter right back.

"Lehman, Thanks for the refund, but he's not for sale. I love this mutt."

The next day, I dug into Sparky's cage satchel and found another piece of paper. Unfolding it I read, "Diploma of Graduation from Lehman's Rocky Mountain Obedience School, Dallas Texas. Sparky Watson, graduated Bachelor of Arts, summa cum laud, 2014."

Then another piece fell out. "Ezra, send that smart dog back next month and we'll finish him off with a doctorate in lead and fetch."

Well, it's not likely that he is going to get a doctorate degree. He might be a lot smarter than me, but there's no way I'm going to call him Dr. Sparky.

After the shock of receiving Lehman's certificate, Sparky and I decided to go fishing. Just to do something different, we drove to the coast and put our boat in at Mercer Lake. This pond was about a mile long and a little over ¼ mile wide. We went trolling. Pretty soon, I hooked a big fat rainbow trout. Sparky bailed out of the boat to get himself a fish. Sparky can't tell a keeper from a throwback. This'un was a keeper though – two more and we'd have us a mess of fish for supper.

Lehman thinks this dog is smart... well, he ain't. When I sent him forward to get me a bass plug, he brought back a Wedding Ring spinner. I wanted to switch lures, but that stupid mutt didn't know the difference between a Crazy Crawler and a Wedding Ring spinner.

"Sparky, you better wise up or I'll ship you right back to Lehman's Rocky Mountain dog school, for more learnin."

The next time I asked for a lure, old Sparky just stood there, waiting for me to describe it. You see, Sparky is just a tad bit color-blind. So I said, "Pooch, will you get me that wooden plug with wings?"

He trotted right over to the tackle box and then pulled out the Crazy Crawler.

"Dumb dog, do I have to explain every little detail?"

When we got home, I was seething. I promptly shipped him off again to Lehman's Dog Training School. Inside his pen I included a letter. "Lehman, either learn this dog some sense or don't send him back. I need a huntin' and fishin' buddy. He doesn't seem to know the difference between a Crazy Crawler and a Wedding Ring spinner. He has no idea what a Crocodile trolling lure is either."

Three days later, when coming home from work, I heard the phone ringing. It was Lehman.

"Hey Ezra, I'm making great progress with, Sparky. He's doing better than expected, but this time, why don't you give me two more months so I can polish him off. It will cost you, but it'll be worth the money."

"OK, I'll trust you, but I feel as if I'm just pouring money down a rat hole."

This time it cost me another $300, but what the heck, Lehman's my brother.

Finally, the day arrived. Sparky was coming home. With eagerness and anticipation, I met the train to pick up my buddy.

What a shock. There he was, no cage and no leash. Sparky was sitting on the platform at attention with a big grin.

Walking up to him, I asked, "What's the big deal Spark?"

He raised his paw and pointed to his collar. I looked and there, engraved on a metal plate, was his name, "Doctor Sparky Watson, LFD."

"So you got a doctorate in lead and fetch. Well, just don't you be getting uppity on me."

Now I do have to call him "Dr. Sparky." If I don't, he pouts. I think I'm being manipulated.

The very next morning was Monday. I got up, put my work jeans on and lo and behold, there by my chair sat my work boots. Every morning before going to work, Dr. Sparky would fetch my boots. When I came home from work and took them off, he would put them away.

Saturday rolled around and then while getting my fishing vest, he lugged in my waders. Once on the lake, I mumbled to myself, "I'd like to catch a bass this morning."

That dog dragged my tackle box over. I opened it and reached for my Crazy Crawler. Dr. Sparky stood over the box shaking his head in disgust. He then raised his paw and pointed to a long slender yellow plug with three sets of treble hooks. Against my better judgment, I went with his choice. We had our limit of bass in less than thirty minutes. Later, while reaching for my boat trolling rod, Sparky had a Crocodile trout lure for me. That dog was amazing, he could read my mind.

Next morning when I got up, I found old Dr. Sparky busy shining my loafers, getting me ready for church. While in the shower, he laid out my suit, tie, shirt and loafers. I don't know if Dr. Sparky wants to be my fishing buddy or my mother.

I am so pleased with that mutt, I think I'll send Lehman another $50 for his trouble.

• • • • • • • • • •

Mario Myatt
January 22, 1934 - July 9, 2015

Rest in Peace, Mario!

When Mario first contacted us in 2010, he sent several children's stories. They were obviously written by someone with a vivid imagination and a child-like sense of humor with few writing skills. He admitted to being a storyteller -- he told these original stories to his grandchildren as they sat upon his knee. Later he wrote the following:

"I am amazed and well-pleased at the attention you've given to the stories I have submitted. I just started writing just this last September, and I am 77 years old. Hardly no education, but am finding that I like to put stuff on paper."

We didn't print those first few stories. They were just too rough. I suggested that he join a writer's group, and I believe that he did. Mario continued to take the suggestions and criticisms that came his way and his writing kept improving. My personal all-time favorite is "Fred Bigfoot" published in the Spring 2013 issue.

How sad we were to learn that he had passed. You will truly be missed, Mario!

pe

Birthdays
By Vicki Sourdry

Today is my birthday. I fear it will be my last.

The first one I really remember is my fifth. We were all on lock-down because of turbulence from an ion storm. My mother had planned a party with some of the other kids on the colony ship, but they were all stuck in their grav-beds, just like I was... and everyone else on the ship. I was so disappointed I cried the whole day. Being five, I didn't understand why it was important to stay in our grav-beds and not move around the ship; I just knew it ruined my birthday party. I learned a couple years later, when my little brother got out of bed during a lock-down and was crushed when the ship turned quickly to miss an asteroid. Hard lesson.

A lot has happened since then.

The second birthday that comes to mind was my twelfth. It was when I was accepted as a man on the ship. The captain always gave a speech, the same speech, when one of us became an adult. She talked about responsibility and duty and work. It didn't sound like much fun, and it wasn't. I no longer went to school. I just worked, hard. I spent every day growing food in the hydroponics bay. Every adult worked making the ship a viable community. We all had to or we wouldn't survive to make it to a habitable planet. You see, the one we were supposed to colonize turned out not to have an atmosphere we could breathe. So the ship had to keep going, looking for another planet. That was when my great-grandparents were young, almost 100 years ago. They were supposed to be the pioneers on Gloria, in the tenth of more than a planned 50 colony ships to leave Earth to "spread humanity to the stars." Instead, they lived and died on the ship, having children, grandchildren, and great-grandchildren -- never again knowing the feeling of walking under an open sky, or breathing air that moved because of wind, or feeling rain on their face.

My twentieth birthday was memorable, to all of us. The captain announced we had found a habitable planet. Before my twenty-second birthday, we were orbiting Gift. We had named it that because that is exactly what it was – the gift of a planet that would allow us to land, create our colony, and fulfill the destiny of our ancestors. Every one of my nearly six thousand shipmates knew that they had a future off the ship. The mood on the ship changed dramatically, from dogged survival to hopeful expectation. The preparation for embarkation continued well past my birthday. The work was different, and even harder, but it was done with light hearts and much joy.

I celebrated my twenty-fifth birthday moving out of the initial colony dormitory onto our own small farm. I was a farmer, married, and a new father. Now my family could grow and thrive, just like the colony was doing. Gift was surpassing our expectations.

My thirty-fifth birthday was spent in mourning. My wife and three children were dead, as were my parents and my sister and her family, and almost half the colony. The plague had started about two years before. It always began with a fever and progressed into seizures and eventually, death. There was nothing anyone could do. Anyone who got sick, died; and no one knew why. Some people got sick, some people didn't. The colony fell into chaos. People became hermits even though it wasn't contagious. Everyone was scared. The schools closed. The factories closed. The shops closed. Many people left the town to fend for themselves. I lived off the food in my fields and tended the graves of my family. Some people blamed each other, which was stupid. Some people blamed God. That was stupid too. Others blamed the planet. As if it had a mind of its own. But no one stood up and tried to bring us together. There was no leadership. All of the original colony leaders had died – the luck of the draw.

When my food had almost run out and the season turned, I took what I could carry from the house and struck out going east. A few had gone this way, but most who had left had gone south where we had just begun to explore before the plague. I wanted nothing to do with any of them. I wanted to be alone with my grief. It was overwhelming. My family had died, but more than that, my dream, and the dream of my ancestors was dying as well.

I struggled in the east. I found a plot of land, and planted seeds I had brought, but the land was not good for crops, and I reaped almost nothing for all my work. I moved to a different place, but still no luck. I saw no one, which was fine, for a while. By my thirty-ninth birthday, I was nearly starving. Game was scarce, and I knew the local flora would barely sustain me for another year. My grief had subsided, and I longed for human companionship. I headed west again.

Just before my fortieth birthday, I returned to Lawson, the town we had built when we landed. It was the only real town on Gift, as far as I knew. I entered on Main Street. A few people saw me and hurried to get inside, turning to look out of windows. No one spoke to me. I kept walking until I got to the elementary school where my kids had gone. It was locked up tight and looked as if it hadn't been used since I left, five years prior. I walked to my farm, the house I had lived in with my wife and kids, where they were buried. A twinge of grief welled up in my chest, threatening to overwhelm my desire for normalcy. I willed it to the recesses of my mind. It never completely left me, I didn't want it to, but it no longer dominated my thoughts. With my resolve finally returned, I opened the front door. It was just as I left it, dust and cobwebs coated surfaces, but nothing had been moved or used. People had died here. No one wanted to take the chance.

On my forty-first birthday, I married Gwen, ten years my junior. We had met just after my last birthday, when I returned to Lawson. She had lost everyone, just like I had. We shared grief and hope for the future, and fell in love. The whole town came to our wedding. All four hundred of them. Four hundred. That's all that was left in the town that had boasted almost 7500 people when the plague had started. About 5000 had died. The rest had left, like I had. We had no idea how many of them were still alive. The dying had stopped three years ago. The stopping was as strange as the starting. No one knew why, it just stopped. People had started coming out of their self-imposed isolation after about a year, but were still wary of strangers coming into town -- fearful that they might bring the plague back. My theory was that everyone who was left now was somehow immune. Those who were going to die, already had. But I worried about children. If we had more, would they be immune? Or would they get sick and die? No one in Lawson had gotten pregnant since the plague started.

On my forty-second birthday, we found out we were going to have a baby. Fear and hope battled within me. I can only imagine what Gwen was going through. We had talked about it. If there were no children, the colony would die out with our generation. We had to try. I think others in town were waiting to see what happened when our baby was born. She was beautiful, and healthy, and she stayed healthy. By my forty-fourth birthday, there were several new additions to our little town. They were all healthy, even though we had no doctors and no medicines. The doctors had died, and all the medicines we had were used to try to fight the plague. None of them had worked, of course, but they were gone. I had started farming again as soon as I came back to Lawson, and now I could barter with everyone else for things they made, or grew, or shot, or caught. We were a healthy bunch, and by my fiftieth birthday, our 400 had grown to nearly 500, including a dozen or so people who had returned from the south and east, craving companionship and community. We found out that many of those who left had died – many from the plague, some from accidents, some from starvation, and a few from suicide. For the most part, we all got along. There was the occasional squabble, of course, but we assigned "neutral mediators" to settle those.

By my sixtieth birthday, Gwen and I had seven kids and had cleared and planted more land, producing even more food for the growing colony. I felt good, and I still worked all day in the fields, along with several of my kids. Our first "baby," Samantha, was now 18 and married to a fine young man who had a small ranch, raising an indigenous flightless bird. We bartered with them, vegetables for meat, on a regular basis.

By my sixty-first birthday, I was a grandfather to a healthy baby boy named Ashton. They had named him after my great grandfather, who was supposed to have been a colonist on Gloria. By now, all the materials from the ship had been used. Nothing had been wasted – not a bolt, not a shred of cloth, not a seed. But our education had been minimal, and we lost most of our skills when the artisans and mechanics and teachers died. We were surviving, but we were not advancing. It worried me that our children, and their children, would have to "invent" things that we should have known already. But we lived well enough. And everyone was living longer. Several had made it to 100 already, and the only reason people died was because of accidents.

By my seventieth birthday, I had seven grandkids, from three of our kids. The other four were still living with Gwen and I, helping us run and expand, the farm. Our hair had turned gray, but we had none of the maladies of "old age" that I remember from the elders on the ship. I still worked in the fields. We danced at community parties. We played with the grandchildren. We enjoyed life.

We had a party on my hundredth birthday. Quite a family we had produced. There were fifty (and a half!) of us. I still got around well, and still spent some time in the fields, but now it was more for fun and exercise. The kids, grandkids, and great grandkids were in charge of the farm, doing most of the actual work. Inventions had come like clockwork in Lawson over the last 50 years – energy for electricity, machines to make things we needed, machines to make farm work easier and more productive, printing so we could share news and information, machines so we could communicate (someone even took one of these to Hawkins, a small community in the south that we found out about from a returning colonist), herbal medicines from plants on Gift (though we didn't seem to need much), all sorts of things that made life easier and more enjoyable. By now there were artists, and musicians, and actors, and writers. There were weavers, and tanners, and makers of all sorts of things. There were farmers, and ranchers, and hunters. Finally, people had begun dying off at about 120 years of age. The plague was a distant memory for the old people, and ancient history for everyone else in the colony. Somehow, it had strengthened those of us who survived so we did not get sick, and lengthened our lives to the human maximum, giving us the best chance to create a stable and thriving colony. It had cost us dearly in the lives of our loved ones, but in the end had been a positive force for us all.

Now, I'm celebrating my 120th birthday. Hard to imagine, really. I have lived through so much change. Ship and colony; heartache and joy; fear and hope; failure and success; grief and love; solitude and community. Our brood has grown to over 100 people, just from Gwen and I!

Lawson has grown and is thriving, and some people have left to start their own communities. It looks like Gift is going to be home to humans for the foreseeable future, and that makes me feel good. I have lived longer than I ever thought I would, but I still feel good, and I'm not ready to go yet.

Trouble is, no one has lived until 121. Gwen is 110, and still beautiful. I visited the graves of my earlier family yesterday. I have never forgotten them, and I don't understand why I survived while none of them did, but I built a life to honor what all of them would have wanted, had they lived.

Well, time for me to go to my last birthday party.

Photo Gallery

Controversial UFO sighting near Roswell, New Mexico *on July 8, 1947. Photo from the October 29, 2013 issue of Beevoz -- ¿Qué ocurrió en Roswell?*

Mother Shopping
By Terah Van Dusen

Years pass and it's still just Dad and me. He's writing letters to single Hare Krishna women who live in places like Sarasota, Florida and Vancouver B.C. The woman in Sarasota sends a photograph. She is full-bodied and dark. In the picture she stands with a man on each arm. I wonder if that is somehow supposed to be alluring. I am too young to know a word like that.

My Dad says he's searching for a mother for me. He figures one of the women he's writing with will move into our cabin and, if we're lucky, cook beans and rice and cauliflower samosas, like Al's wife does. Slowly the letters stop coming and my Dad doesn't mention the women again.

In the winter, like an act of God, Suzanne comes into our life. Suzanne is a Christian woman my dad meets at my Christian Preschool, Grace Lutheran—where I'm always getting in trouble for giggling and poking boys during naptime. Suzanne's son, Cameron, goes there. He is one year younger than me and not as rough as the neighborhood boys up the river. He's the kind of kid who might tell on you, but other than that, he's harmless.

No one can figure what a beautiful woman like Suzanne is doing dating my dad. But I can see that she likes him for the same reason everyone else does: Adventure. My Dad takes me, Suzanne and Cameron on long hikes, rain or shine, to places like Strawberry Lake and Madhatter's Gorge. Suzanne knows these excursions are what Cameron needs and has been missing. Cameron's Dad, like my Mom, lives who-knows-where and we all know too little about them to ever bring them up in conversation.

Our family holds its breath as a few short years of Dad and Suzanne pass. Cameron and I do well together—though I am more like the little boy and he is more like the little girl. We even bathe together until I kick him straight in his naked "junk" just to see what will happen. Of course, he cries and tells on me.

Suzanne never gets too close to me. I don't think she wanted to get too attached. Once, she brushes my long wet hair and dresses me in her clean gray stretch pants and oversized t-shirt. She pats my butt tenderly, a small motherly gesture, and feeds Cameron and I lovely kid freezer food (the kind I rarely get to eat) on plastic placemats in front of the television while my Dad and her go into the bedroom and shut the door behind them. I know what they're doing in there but don't saying anything to Cameron because I know he won't understand.

I thought because they were lying together in the bedroom kissing and rolling around that things were going well. I thought that maybe Cameron would become my brother. I decide that if Cameron doesn't become my brother, well then someday I will marry him.

I can only guess as to what exactly happened between my Dad and Suzanne. My guess would be that my Dad was too nice a guy and that nice guys finish last. Or maybe it was religion that came between them. We all saw it coming. Maybe that was the problem, in and of itself.

Or it could have been one of any number of other things: Suzanne and her tidy little red house on Birch Street; her good job at the dentist's office; her grace and her stability; her prissy (though well-intentioned) son who would eventually go to the only private school in the county.

Or, were there other reasons?... my dad and his cabin with one window and a rope for a door handle; his decent job at the road department where everyone thought he was crazy, but really he was just passionate and free-thinking; his doll of a five-year-old that made everyone think "How Sad For Them."

And so we went on living without a mother, and we were OK.

Photo Gallery

Groundwaters' own Jennifer Chambers as a baby at her grandparents' home in Santa Cruz, California, about 1976.

A Tale of Two Fish
By Ron Veneski

Tom took his girlfriend's father, Gus, fishing. Upon their return from the river, while Tom checked the boat and trailer hitch to insure the connection to the truck was still secure, Gus took the only fish they caught, a 29 inch, 5½ pound salmon, to show his wife and kids, telling them that he caught it.

Annie, Tom's girlfriend greeted him as he started toward the house. "My dad is really proud of that fish that he caught."

Tom asked "What fish? He didn't catch any fish. I did."

"What?"

"That's right, we only landed one fish today and that is the one your dad took into the house."

Annie could see the anger building in Tom as he started toward the house. She grabbed him by the arm.

"What are you going to do," she asked.

"I'm going in there to set the record straight."

"Please don't, he will be upset and embarrassed."

Tom saw the look of concern on Annie's face and agreed to say nothing, but vowed to get even.

As Tom entered the kitchen, Gus was elaborating even more on this big lie.

Gus turned to Tom held up the fish and said "It's a beauty isn't it Tom? Not bad for a guy who knows nothing about fishing, can't swim and is fearful of drowning?"

Tom responded with "Great catch Gus, great catch. We'll have to go again soon."

Tom took Annie by the hand and headed for the front door. Stopping by the truck, Annie could feel the tension between them.

"You're mad aren't you?" Annie said.

"No I'm not mad or angry, I'm just about ready to explode. He is going to pay for what he did and will regret this incident for a long time."

"Are you really that upset?"

"Yes, because he crossed the line again today as he has many times in the past and keeps getting away with it. Somebody needs to put a stop to this and I'm willing to step up and do it."

"He will not take this well at all."

"Annie, he needs to feel what it's like when somebody is on the receiving end of all the lies and verbal abuse he lays on other people. Let the battle begin."

Annie stood on the driveway as Tom pulled away. She was torn between two allegiances – struggling with who she was hoping would win.

Tom headed home to clean up the boat and other equipment. The audacity of Gus was still banging around in his head and needed to be addressed. Gus was going to pay, he would see to that. Tom needed a plan of attack and he knew exactly who to turn to for help.

Tom called his two fishing buddies, telling them he had a problem he needed to discuss with them. Word got out to others and all met at the local pizza joint where various solutions were discussed. One by one each member of the group offered a suggestion. None met with the entire group's approval until Doc spoke.

"Here is the problem as I see it" replied Doc. We need to beat Gus at his own game and make sure he never does this again."

Doc's plan was simple. Tom needed to "catch" a bigger fish than the one Gus had claimed for his "own" and show him up. The problem was that salmon season was closing in seven days. Everyone understood that it didn't matter who caught the fish, it would go to Tom so he could claim that he caught it.

Three days later Tom went to Annie's house to watch a football game on TV. Greeted by Gus at the door, he was ushered into the family room where the rest of the family was already watching the game. Gus, smiling from ear to ear asked if he noticed anything different. Tom knew what he meant, but chose to ignore it. Gus pointed with pride to the picture of him holding the fish he claimed to have caught. Tom managed a faint smile of approval and sat down to watch the game. The picture was going to be hard to miss because Gus mounted it on the wall right behind the TV.

Gus was his usual self during the game, challenging every call by the refs officiating the game and questioning the game plays called by the coaches of both teams. He was really in his element and continued his obnoxious ways until the game ended.

Only four days remained for Tom and his friends to catch a suitable fish.

This has got to work, Tom thought to himself. I can't take his crap for a whole year before I can catch a bigger fish than the one Gus stole from me. Maybe I'm making too much out of this whole incident and it's not worth the effort, but Gus has pulled stunts like this too often and it has to stop.

Tom vowed to continue regardless of what the outcome might be.

The next meeting with Tom's friends was on Friday night and fishing season closed the following day. The outlook wasn't promising. No one had any good news and the hope that tomorrow would bring better news was fading. Rather than let the whole night be ruined, Tom ordered pizza and beer for the whole group and said he was picking up the tab. All accepted the offer and commented on how much better it tasted when it was free.

When it appeared that everyone had their fill of pizza and beer, someone suggested they order one more round.

Tom groaned and said, "It's amazing how much more pizza you guys can eat when someone else is paying for it."

Laughter erupted along with comments like, "Free is always better" and "I hope you brought your credit card and cash."

When it was announced that pizza order number 52 was ready, Doc sauntered up to the counter to pick it up. What he brought back, however, was not pizza but rather a 7 pound, 33 inch salmon lying on a bed of ice. Tom was dumbfounded and all the guys were laughing and whooping it up.

The plan was beginning to fall into place. Tom called Annie the next day and asked her to come over to his place. He said he needed some help with a project he was working on.

"Okay, what is this project all about?" asked Annie when she arrived.

Tom said, "Go look inside the ice chest on the kitchen floor."

Annie lifted the lid and couldn't believe what she saw.

"Wow, that's a beauty," she replied.

Tom said, "I want to take a few pictures of me holding this fish, then I want to take the fish over to your house and show it to Gus. I think we should offer to fix it for dinner tonight while it is still fresh."

"You know my dad is not going to like this at all don't you?"

"I do, but did he expect me to like the fact that he stole my fish and told everybody in this house that he caught it? I don't think so."

Pictures were taken and preparations were made to go to Annie's house. She had already called ahead and told her mother that she would bring all the fixings for dinner.

"That's great because everyone groaned when I mentioned spaghetti as a possibility," her mother said.

On the drive over Annie was unusually quiet, and the silence didn't go unnoticed by Tom who reached over and tapped her shoulder.

"What's wrong?" Tom asked.

"I'm concerned about how my dad is going to react to all of this."

"Gus is a big boy and should be able to handle it. And, who knows, this may even help him improve his social skills. God knows they could use some improving."

Upon entering the house, Tom was delighted to see that everyone was home – Mom, Gus and Annie's two brothers – perfect.

Gus eyed the cooler as Tom set it down on the kitchen floor, but didn't utter a word.

Annie's mom asked, "What's in the cooler?"

Tom replied, "I thought you would never ask," and reached into the cooler and removed the fish. He held it up so the fish was displayed full length so everyone could see it.

"Wow, that is a nice fish! Annie call the boys. They are in their bedroom playing video games."

The boys were impressed and exuberant when they saw the fish and immediately commented. "Dad that fish is even bigger than the one you caught a couple of weeks ago. Great catch Tom."

Gus walked out of the kitchen without commenting and went back to watching the football game on TV.

The family feasted on the fish for dinner without any more drama. Afterwards Tom and Annie left for his house so she could pick up her car.

After Annie left, Tom looked at the pictures that Annie had taken of him holding the fish. Deliberately he had struck a pose similar to that of Gus showing off "his" fish. He then headed off to get it framed.

The next evening, Tom drove to Annie's house for a planned movie date. He showed the picture to Annie, the boys, and then to Annie's mom who immediately suggested hanging it next to Gus' picture in the family room. Gus wanted to protest but he knew he was outnumbered. Tom's picture was going up on the wall.

Annie excused herself to finish putting on her makeup and fixing her hair. Tom joined Gus in the family room.

"Well Gus, welcome to the club."

Gus looked over at Tom and said, "What club are you talking about?"

Tom replied, "The Liars Club."

"Are you nuts, I never joined anything called The Liars Club."

"Sure you did," said Tom. "It happened the day I took you fishing and you brought the fish I caught into the house and told everybody that you caught it."

Tom continued, "Now I have some news for you. I didn't catch the fish that I am holding in the picture either. But, I have seven fishing buddies who will swear that they were there and saw me catch it."

Gus blurted out, "That's not fair."

"Not fair, really? Then what you did must not be fair either!

Tom waited for him to respond, but Gus remained silent.

"Bubbling Up" Fiction

(From our talented under-18 contributors)

The Haunted House
By Natalie Edwards

One Halloween night Layla and Frank did not want to go trick or treating, so their Mom said, "You should go to the new haunted house." So they said, "O.K.!"

When they got there, they gave them a flashlight in case the power went out.

The first things they saw were two signs. One said "Little Kid Place" and the other said, "Entrance." They went to the entrance. When they went into the first door, they saw a walking mummy. They jumped! When they went to the next door, there was nothing, so they stood for a second, and all of a sudden, a ton of mummies and zombies came out of the ground. They screamed and then went to the next door. There was a sign that said "Beware of bats."

"That's crazy! Why would they put live bats in a building!" Frank said.

So, they went in and there were bats everywhere! They screamed.

They ran to the next door when the power went out. Layla yelled, "Turn on the flashlight Frank!"

"I can't! It's broken!

Ten minutes later they said, "Our phones have lights!" So, they got out their phones and got out of the haunted house.

When they got home, they told their mom the whole story. She said, "Do you want to go next year?"

Then they screamed,
"YES!"

Lucy and Sierra's Halloween
By Natalie Edwards

Chapter I - The Pumpkin Patch

Lucy and Sierra are very beautiful people. They are a brilliant orange and ... Did I say "people?" Sorry, I meant pumpkins. Anyway, they were stunning and they never wanted to be separated. So one day a family came to the patch and they looked at Lucy and they said that she was ugly. Then they looked at Sierra and said that she was perfect. So they took Sierra and they left Lucy.

Lucy was freaking out, wondering what she was going to do without Sierra. While they put Sierra in the car, she was so happy to be picked that she forgot all about Lucy. Meanwhile, another family came along and chose Lucy. When they put her in the back of the car, there was a ton of sweaty boy pumpkins trying to act all tough. When Lucy got to the house, there were a lot of big animals that could crush the pumpkins. In her mind, Lucy screamed. There was a For Sale sign and a ton of boxes all around. They set her on a pile of boxes.

Meanwhile Sierra got to her new house. It was a 3-story mansion. There were a mom, dad, and one child named Mcylee. They were so rich that that was the 10th time they went to the pumpkin patch in the last two weeks. So there was at least 20 pumpkins, at most 50. After Sierra finished admiring all of her potential friends, she started listening to their conversation.

" Mommy! Can we get another pumpkin tomorrow so we can put one in every room?"

"Maybe, Sweetheart. We are going to greet our new neighbors and show them around the neighborhood."

While they carried on their conversation Sierra thought about who the neighbors would be. Would it be Lucy? No it couldn't be Lucy. Why would it be?

Chapter 2 - The Houses

Lucy, on the other hand was wondering where they were moving to. Is it going to be Paris, New York, China, Russia?!!

"What am I going to do? What am I going to do?"

All of a sudden, Lucy thought of a great idea. Sit on my side like I'm going to fall, then they'll put me on the ground and when they're not looking, move closer and closer to their closing papers to see where the house is. She went along with her plan, and it worked. It wasn't as bad as she thought, because they set her down right next to the papers on the step. She read it and it was 227 Elmore Street, Creswell, OR. She was so happy that it was not Paris, New York, China, or Russia, and besides, it is only an hour or so away from their current location. She was still wondering who they would be moving next to. She was still thinking about it when the car pulled out of the driveway.

When they came back, at least a half an hour later, they set down even more papers next to Lucy. She read them. It said that the neighbors are Lucas, Marilyn, and Mcylee Edgerton. But that did not give her any more clues about who their pumpkin was.

But wait a second. When I was at the pumpkin patch, a little girl and her parents, Marilyn and Lucas, called her ugly. It all made sense now. She was moving in next to Sierra. She was so excited, she could scream! But, wait! I won't see her unless they carve together. What is happening? What is happening?

Chapter 3 - The Humpfreys Meet the Edgertons

Sierra was still wondering who else was moving next to them and if they had a pumpkin. I still think that it might be Lucy, but that would be a dumb coincidence. Two days later, it was moving day for the Humpfrey family. A week later they were moved in the day before Halloween. An hour after the Humpfrey family moved in, the Edgerton family came to show them around. While the grown-ups talked, the 3 kids talked about ponies, rainbows and unicorns.

Anyway, back to the parents, they were talking about carving pumpkins together. Lucy's family said that they might carve a few of their pumpkins before, or after they come over to carve because they have so many people and pumpkins in their family. While Sierra listened to that she wanted to scream. So many thoughts were going through her head. Would Lucy be carved with me? Will I ever see her again? Is she ok? Five minutes later, the Humpfrey family went inside with at least five sweaty boy pumpkins, and to Lucy's relief, not her.

An hour later they were done carving. They came over to the Edgerton's house to carve their six other pumpkins, including Lucy. She was so excited to see Sierra, she could scream! When they got inside they set Lucy and the other pumpkins down on the newspaper with 7 other pumpkins and waited for the people to come back to carve them .

When Lucy looked at the crowd of the Edgerton's pumpkins, she couldn't see Sierra. She was freaking out. Then the people came back and moved their pumpkins and finally she saw Sierra. The families chose their templates for the carvings. Most of them were scary, but Lucy and Sierra's were happy and joyful. It took them an hour to carve all the pumpkins, but they succeeded to carve all of them. In the end the Edgerton family had so many pumpkins that they wanted to share with the Humpfrey's. In the end they gave them 20 pumpkins, Including Sierra. In all, Lucy was happy that she and Sierra were together for Halloween.

Photo Gallery

The Creswell covered bridge, over the Coast Fork of the Willamette River in Lane County, was built by L. N. Roney in 1884. The photo was taken shortly after completion and shows former Governor John Whiteaker, who died in 1903, at left with a longcoat and pipe. The legend at the top of the bridge reads: "$25 fine for riding - driving over bridge faster than a walk; $25 fine for driving over 10 head cattle - horses across at one time." The bridge was 140 feet long and was a Howe truss. It was replaced in 1931 after approximately 47 years of use.

The following horror story is being included in the "Bubbling Up" section because it was written and submitted to Groundwaters by a young man who was still a senior in high school in 2012. While we felt Hayden had a natural writing talent, we were uncomfortable with the violence this story contains. We have since decided, however, that it merits an audience.

The Hunted
By Hayden Larsen

It is coming! Running as fast as the wind blows! I cry out as I run through the streets hoping beyond hope that my screams will be heard and that I will be saved from the thing that is after me. But I know that my hopes are for nothing.

While I'm running, a horrible scream of maniacal laughter mixed with the sound of the pattering of clawed feet erupts from behind me. As I run down a dark alley in hopes of evading the creature behind me, my hopes are shattered as I see, to my horror, that I have come upon a dead end... No one will ever find me, even my very bones will not be found and the only one that will know shall be him, "The Eye."

As I turn around to face the nightmare behind me, I see nothing at first, then a shadow comes across the alley as I finally see what I have been running from.

The creature stands almost nine feet tall on two muscular legs that house three clawed toes. Its head is hideously deformed and dome-shaped, but nothing startled me more than the eye. It was filled with both insanity and pure evil, but there was also a gleam that suggested that its life was made up of tragedy and something else, hidden beneath its grotesque form. The wide mouth that was filled with razor sharp thin, needle-like teeth, was almost transfixed into a psychotic smile and its two long, extremely muscular arms, ended in four long dagger-like claws that could rip a man in two with incredible ease. On each of the elbows were long sharp spikes.

The creature's skin was crusty in texture and blood-red in color; nearly its whole body was covered in blood, some of which dripped from its body like rain. Its body was covered in an assortment of scars on its chest and it had a long scar across its eye. His eye was fixated on me now; starring into my soul. The beast's mouth changed into a malevolent smile as it thought of what it would do to me. Then it took a step closer... and another... and yet another. Its shuffling changed into a run, then bounding, it jumped in the air, grabbing with its long talons onto the concrete walls that were sandwiching both of us. It repeated the same technique as it leaped from wall to wall, all the while laughing manically.

I had no time to scream, I groped around for a door handle to a hidden passageway to escape the fate that awaits me, and I find none. I close my eyes as if that would save me from my fate as the creature leaped towards me, talons shining in the moonlight and drool oozing from the corners of its mouth before splashing onto the ground. Seconds passed by as I waited for my demise; when nothing happened, I opened my eyes. He was standing in front of me, a malicious smile transfixed on his face. It was then that the beast spoke. A voice that sounded like two people talking at the same time in an eerie echoing voice, "You really think that you can escape from your destiny? Now that's so sad, it is almost touching. But now I'm going to kill you and no one in this sad little world will mourn you."

It then let out a maniacal laugh that sent chills to my very bones. Suddenly there was a blinding flash of pain erupting from my chest, a blinding flash of light and a sense of comfort came over me as I reached towards the light as it faded into permanent darkness.

Photo Gallery

"Contemplation." Jim Burnett, Sr. (aka Jimminy Cricket) obviously trying to ignore his little sister, Patty, while camping and picnicking (ca 1949).

Groundwaters

Non-Fiction

Non-Fiction

Table of Contents

Photo Gallery

The Old Lane County Courthouse in Eugene as seen in 1958. Lane County was created January 28, 1851, by the territorial legislature. *Photo courtesy of the Ben Maxwell Collection #3434, Salem Public Library Historic Photograph Collections, Salem Public Library, Salem, Oregon.*

The Durbin Line - A Memoir
By Mary Alexander

My family, the Durbins, migrated north from Los Angeles in 1939, one the last years of the Great Depression. That summer my Dad was 33 years old, Mama, 30, my brother Maurice (known generally as "Marty") was 12, sister Peggy June, 10 (she later dropped Peggy and was only known as "June"), and yours truly, Mary Lou, 4. ("Lou" was short for Louise, but I dropped that to settle for just "Mary".)

I deeply admire the courage it took for my folks to journey north, not knowing a soul in Oregon and having only their own determination as their strongest resource.

By the spring of 1940 Dad proposed that they purchase a ten-acre plot of ground in the Silk Creek area a few miles west of Cottage Grove.

To persuade Mama, Dad said," Berenice, the house is kinda rough, but it has water inside and a good cook stove. There's plenty of firewood to be cut right on the property. The barn can keep more than one cow. It's got a large field that's been cleared to grow hay and alfalfa, and there's a good garden plot. We'll be able to grow everything we eat."

Mama, ever pragmatic, countered, "Bill, it may be the best we can do right now, but I won't be without electricity. This is the 20th century, and I've put up with kerosene lamps as long as I'm going to. If you promise to get electricity for us, I'll go along with it."

So electricity became Daddy's first priority. It was not a small challenge for him.

Meantime, Mama scrubbed, polished, and painted every surface in the house, in addition to setting up a chicken coop, inhabiting it with a fearless rooster and a harem of Rhode Island Reds. Every morning and evening Mama milked our cow, Tilly. Peggy was assigned the job of cleaning the cream separator Mama acquired so she could sell the excess cream that we didn't consume ourselves.

Marty set about building a pig pen and installing a young boar. That boar later became a source of family amusement because he only stayed in the pen at night or while Marty was in school. The rest of the time he followed Marty at his chores all around our little farm. We knew when Marty was in the out house; there would be Sam, patiently waiting outside the door.

Peggy June and Marty had a bit of a discussion over the garden. She said, "I shouldn't have to do the digging because I have to clean the separator and I have all the dishes to do after dinner."

Marty insisted, "I have a lot more chores than you do. How would you like to shovel the cow poop from the barn? You wanna slop Sam's trough?"

However, he was conscripted for the tilling of the garden plot. Peggy June and Mama did the planting and weeding.

Dad bought a plow horse, Nelly, to turn the soil for the alfalfa field. Marty was expected to feed and care for Nelly.

As the youngest, and probably the most inept, my chores were pretty modest. Until we got electricity, I had to clean the kerosene lamp chimneys. My hands were small enough to fit inside these easily. I was expected to make the bed I shared with my sister. I was supposed to dry the evening's dinner dishes, but I often escaped that task by falling asleep by the heating stove in the living room. At this late date I'm willing to admit, I sometimes faked it, and I would hear Mama say, "Let her sleep. She helped me by picking and cleaning the berries we had for supper."

I took care of our dog Corky, as he was my special companion while I roamed the ten acres. He was a beautiful canine cross between an Irish setter and golden cocker spaniel, and I loved him dearly.

Dad was up before daylight and off to his paying job for the Oregon, Pacific, and Eastern Railroad. The long hours made it hard for him to make good on his promise to Mama that he would get electricity to our house. Our mail address was a box on Lorane Route. The highway from Cottage Grove to Lorane had power lines running beside it, but they did not extend to our little Silk Creek road. What Dad had to do was poll everyone who lived along our road from the highway to the last house up the mountain, and get them to sign his petition to bring the power all the way up. He didn't expect it to be a problem. Surely everybody wants electricity, he thought.

The old couple who lived just a little down the hill from us, the Overholsers, were in their 80's, still living on their own, and had done very well, thank you, for all those eighty years without any new-fangled electricity. They liked Mama and Daddy, but didn't see the need for making a change.

Across the road, and up a bit was the home of young folks, Clara and Clarence Duncan. Clara was the oldest sister of my best friend, Joyce Allen. The Duncans were thrilled with the prospect of getting the power. Clara declared, "The first thing I'm going to get is a radio. It gets so darned lonesome here all day when Clarence is at work."

Clara's family, the Allens, had their farm up at the end of the road. Mr. Allen had cleared the land himself and raised his family there. He came down the road every Sunday to lead the services at the little church that served the whole community of the area. The church yard and cemetery were adjacent to the one room school grounds.

Mrs. Allen had a pump organ in their living room. On the rare occasions when I was allowed to go home with Joyce Ann for some play time together, I was thrilled if her mother would play the organ for us. She also played the church's pump organ for services. They had a large comfortable home, but with few modern conveniences.

Like our elderly neighbors, Mr. Allen had trouble seeing any need to spend money to pay for electric power when he had managed well without it. Dad tried to help him see things from his perspective. Daddy had great plans for improving his own property once he had the advantage of electricity. He spoke of powering the well to pump water for a duck pond, and to replace the old hand pump in our kitchen, so all we would have to do is turn on a tap. He mentioned the pleasure of having a radio to keep in touch with what was going on in the country and the world. Perhaps it was Mr. Allen's own daughter, Clara, whose voice made the difference in his final decision to sign on.

I don't remember clearly, but I think the Hanks family lived downhill and across the road from us. Rosemary and Billy Hanks attended the same one-room school that we did. Billy Hanks was in my 1st grade. At any rate, Daddy needed Mr. Hanks' signature, too, on his petition, and was glad when he signed on.

My sister, Peggy June, would visit the Overholser's with occasional gifts of Mama's cooking or baked goods. She would do a little housecleaning for Mrs. Overholser. In appreciation, they would pay her in coins for her efforts. Once I was allowed to accompany her. Mrs. Overholser showed me how to use their stereopticon. I thought it was magic. I had never seen one before, and only in museums since. It made the first 3D pictures. Peggy was very respectful toward these old folks. I don't know if her kindnesses influenced Mr. Overholser to finally agree to Mr. Edison's invention of electricity in his home.

I do know that years later, Joyce Ann Allen married the Overholser's grandson, Connely Overholser, who was my playmate when he visited his grandparents.

Dad ultimately secured all the signatures required. Credit is due to his persuasive skills and determined persistence. The power poles were set in place and lines strung the full length of our road up the hill.

The day the power was turned on was a day for real celebration. Daddy had already set the lines to the house and wired the rooms with sockets and light bulbs. He made good on his promise to Mama. The power company named the tangent from the highway up our road The Durbin Line.

Oregon's Wild and Scenic Rogue River
By Michael J. "Hoss" Barker

(Written for *OREGON'S MAIN STREET: U.S. Highway 99 "The Folk History,"*
Brew and Edwards, 2014)

When asked to write a few paragraphs about the Rogue River, I was at first pleased and eager to start my chore until it dawned on me – how do you write just a few paragraphs about arguably one of the most famous waterways in the nation?

I make no claims to be an authority on the Rogue, but the old girl and I do have a history together, albeit a far too brief one. It was in September 2001, about two weeks or so after 9-11, and I had just secured a job as a handyman at Paradise Lodge, right smack in the middle of the famed 'Wild and Scenic Section.' It was no accident I wound up on the Rogue – I was on a mission to write a book of poetry and short stories about my career as an Oregon logger and Alaska timber tramp, and I was bound and determined to do it where my favorite childhood author, Zane Grey, had a cabin and plied his trade. Getting on at Paradise was fate or providence, however one looks at things like that, as it is about three or four miles downriver from Zane Grey's historically-preserved cabin on the Rogue. I would be there – literally in Paradise – for almost six years – two or three weeks on, and then one week off. There are no roads in the canyon, no phone or power lines; everything comes up on a jet boat and it will forever be that way.

I wasn't long in discovering the allure and majesty of the canyon from the sleepy tidewater with its bucolic and pastoral homesites on the Gold Beach end of the Rogue. There are remarkable geographical similarities as well on the upper stretch in the Medford-Grants Pass area before it enters the Wild and Scenic section.

At Graves Creek, the river loses its homey rock-a-bye baby innocence with the old sway-back cow chewing her cud by the sagging gate, and becomes what could be said as 'schizophrenic,' for lack of a better term.

For the first-timers the river is awe-inspiring, if not terrifying, as you go shooting through boulder-strewn stretches of whitewater with the slate and granite canyon walls towering 1,500 to 2,000 feet on either side. Few places offer such a testament to the power of time, water and gravity as the mighty Rogue carves its way through the Coast Range to seek its end at the Pacific Ocean.

Intermittently, the gauntlet of boulders and whitewater gives way to brief respites of calm, and one can take in the rugged beauty of spartan patches of firs and cedars mingled amongst the dogwoods and madrones, all of them clinging for dear life on the steep, craggy canyon sides. They stand over their fallen forebearers, lying strewn about as nature saw fit to place them, on the hillsides or in the water or piled up in bunches where the angry torrents of winter deluges threw them. There's no rhyme or reason to any of it, as it should be in wild places. They lie among the thousands of silver gray snags, already dead, that await the day they too will fall.

There are the scars of the Silver, Biscuit, and Blossom Complex fires that ravaged the canyon, over the years. I was there for the Biscuit and Blossom fires, ready to don a life jacket and head for Gold Beach if the need arose!

Here and there are a few isolated lodges for river-weary travelers. They are havens where they can actually have a little time to reflect on what they are experiencing and to wonder what the next day will offer.

The seasons provide entirely different experiences for folks. Obviously, summer is the biggest draw and the critters aren't the least bit shy. The old doe and her bouncing fawns will pay you no mind and the big sow bear and her cubs could care less who you are as they tear apart a salmon and bawl like the babies they are. The otters will put on a show for you like they're on the payroll, and if you keep your eyes peeled, you'll see turtles sunning themselves on the rocks and the bald and golden eagles can't help but show off... you would too if you looked that good!

Winter was my favorite time. I had the whole canyon to myself; very rarely do people venture there in the winter. Paradise, at that time, was the only lodge that kept a staff on through the winter. When the rain is persistent and they dump water from Lost Creek Dam into the river, the water can rise 10-feet overnight, and be unsafe to boat on for weeks at a time, as I found out on a few occasions.

Amid all the splendor and beauty, one must always keep in mind that it is the wilderness, and it can be very unforgiving of your mistakes as a few unfortunate folks find out every year – unfortunately, the hard way. Sadly, I was privy to six deaths in my tenure – every one of them a 'freak' incident.

There are a few ways to treat yourself to the Rogue's wild and scenic wilderness area. You can either enter from Grants Pass by taking the Hellsgate jet boat trips or from Gold Beach using Jerry's Rogue Jets or the Mail Boats. I hear they merged a few years back.

For a more peaceful, laid-back trip, there are many experienced river guides to choose from; rafting and fishing trips abound. Go for it! But be careful so that you can live to tell others about it! You'll never forget the experience.

On the Siuslaw River
by Stanley Buck

The old wooden dynamite box stood at the corner of the tent, but it was nearly empty except for a can of condensed milk and two cans of pork and beans. The dog's dish had a chunk of goat meat, and a couple of dry Friskies dog food pellets. Eight feet down the bank was a little sandy beach, and the shallow river flowed over sandstone bedrock and green moss, contrasted by bright red crawdads, and little riffles, winding optimistically toward the ocean, still 80 miles or more away.

It was 1951 and my mom, dad, and I were homeless and living in an old army surplus wall tent in the Siuslaw National Forest, 35 miles from Eugene, Oregon. We had nothing, and yet, we were rich. I was 17, but I didn't feel poor because I had my .22 rifle, and a 1947 Indian Chief motorcycle, much like a big Harley Davidson. The state police owned the bike before me. I parked my Indian next to Dad and Mom's 1941 Chevrolet Master Deluxe coupe. (Master Deluxe meant that it had some extra chrome strips, and nicer hubcaps on the 600 x 16 inch wheels.) Earlier in the day, Dad missed a deer with his .32 Winchester Special. He never was a good shot like me, so there was no fresh meat that day.

Anyway, Mom's job, washing dishes in a restaurant, was rotten because, although she worked her heart out in that sweatshop, the boss was cruel and mean. To work, she had to belong to the union; the union bosses were crooked parasites living off the backs of the workers and they probably got some kickbacks from the management, too. So, Mom quit and Dad had no job either. I had made enough money driving bean stakes, picking cherries, and stacking lumber to buy my motorcycle, but, we had no home.

Living in the old-growth rainforest changes you. Over time, you become a participant, not an observer, with the surroundings. No, it goes even deeper than that. I believe that the primeval "bush spirit" emerges in some of us, and we are actually living in a separate dimension from others. But, it does not stay that way, because when you leave the woods for a couple of years, your "bush spirit" fades away, and you become part of the mundane. (Only a few people know this.)

Down the road in a clearing, lost in time, stood part of a barn, left from a long-abandoned 19th century homestead. It was made of rough hewn wood and had a hay loft and a split shake roof with daylight showing through. I sat up there with my .22 and picked off rabbits and graydiggers, a type of squirrel. They popped up on the hillside that had once been a pasture. Part of the old orchard still stood, and there were marvelous apples, a peculiar old-fashioned variety that exists no more.

In the late afternoon, long shadows crossed the road. Were they evil designs like Gothic symbols, by chance? I left the homestead and headed back for our camp. Uneasy, my bush spirit felt a presence, and I felt a strange chill that was unusual on the warm road in July. Then I heard a metallic ringing sound. Was someone pounding on a pipe? Perhaps a surveyor was driving a stake into the earth's bosom to mark a timber survey. Often, you find a stake like that, usually near the road. It was loud and sounded like it was coming from no more than 20 feet away, but no one was there. Finally my curiosity got the best of me, and I jumped into the brush, waded across the river, and entered the dark forest on the other side in the direction of the sound. It was still as death, and I could hear my own heartbeats between the beats of the iron pipe sound, and it was close, very close. Every time I moved toward it, it changed direction. First, it seemed off to the right; I would go right. Then it was off to the left, and I would look left, but I never could find it. It was loud, and accented by the stillness and quiet of the forest. There was not a trace of anyone or anything... not anything alive, that is. Soon, the sound stopped. There was not a trace of anything there. I went back to camp.

The morning sun shone through the trees and onto the river, making a green and golden light show for me on the ripples. There was no real music, just the sound of the water. So, I went back up the road and crossed int. woods near where I had heard th sound the day before. Birds were chirping, and I could hear a chipmunk cussing me out for getting too close. This was a yum-yum nice morning like a Disney movie. Then, when I reached the spot where the sound had come from, the chill returned, and the woods were silent, strangely silent, and my bush spirit felt like the spot was permeated with evil, even the animals sensed it and shunned the area, I walked around on it and it was only about 50 feet in diameter. There was a subliminal evil presence there. I got out of there. But, since it made no sense, and I was not superstitious, I returned to the place a couple more times on different days to check it out. It was still the same. Very creepy, and I will never go there again. It may have been my imagination, but then sometimes I still have strange dark dreams of that place, 60 years later.

Making Much Out of Little

By Jennifer Chambers

My latest book, *Remarkable Oregon Women: Revolutionaries and Visionaries*, is all about women who have made Oregon, my home state, the place it is today. Due to the space limits, not everything would fit in the book. One of my favorite parts in it—though, like children, you can't really have a favorite—is the section on Pioneering Oregon Women.

My interest started when my mom, a director, directed a play called Quilters. It is a musical with the text (not the music, of course) taken directly from the overland diaries of women crossing the country to a new life. The musical beautifully captures the feelings these women had when they left everything they knew and took their families into the mysterious "West."

The women who went all the way to Oregon on the Oregon Trail faced their own challenges. The floods, famine, terrain challenges, disease, and injury problems that faced every "overlander" were magnified if one didn't hit Independence Rock by July 4. Then it became a race to finish before weather became like its own character in a novel, the unpredictable villain that punished indiscriminately and sometimes with severe consequences. One of the things that is hard to read is the stories of how the travelers treated the Native Americans on the trail, and how they were treated in return. It really makes you wonder if any of the travelers ever stopped to think that they were invading someone else's home. It also makes me wonder how people just took westward progress as a right, which makes me think about the nature of immigration as a whole, even in today's context. It makes the response of Native Americans, when it was negative, more understandable, even though I have no personal experience of their culture.

Take this experience of Pioneer Sarah Wrenn, whose family crossed in 1853:

"When the wagons crossed—the women and children being floated over in wagon-boxes, made waterproof for that purpose—mother and her children were left on the bank, to be carried over later. In the crossing there was trouble with the stock, and other thing of an unforeseen nature happened, and before it was realized darkness had settled down—and there was mother and her little folk, with no food and no protection from the cold, and unfriendly Indians lurking in the background. To attempt to cross the river, cold and swift as it was, in the darkness, was suicide. There was nothing to do but wait till morning, with what feelings may be imagined."

The family remained safe that day and crossed at first light. Later in her story, Sarah tells how another band of Indians came and took her father's hunting knife from his hands as he used it, and tried repeatedly to purchase her older sister, without avail, and she hid under the seat each time they came near a crossing to prevent that from happening again. It is completely understandable that the family would be scared. It's hard to imagine leaving everything and having only the items in your wagon, let alone defending yourself from whatever came at you on the trail. But the negative interactions with Native Americans were actually not the norm, according to my research, but the exception.

Many Native Americans were welcoming. Many helped shepherd the sometimes ignorant Pioneers. Others were able to profit from the trips by helping ford rivers or guide parties around obstacles. I had been vaguely aware of this before I researched Pioneer Diaries, but it was fascinating to me how many tales of help outweighed the stories of attack.

Another interesting thing to me about the Pioneer women was how they ate both on the trail and once they arrived. Of the thousands of pounds of food and supplies most Pioneers carried, much had to be jettisoned.

Lansford Hastings' *Emigrants' Guide to Oregon and California*, published in 1845:

> **"In procuring supplies for this journey, the emigrant should provide himself with, at least, 200 pounds of flour, 150 pounds of bacon; ten pounds of coffee; twenty pounds of sugar; and ten pounds of salt."**

So they were often foragers, or as often as they could be they were. It made me more aware of each berry I picked this year as my family and I collected our blackberries for jam. How did the pioneers preserve them? They couldn't exactly put it up neatly in freezer Ziploc bags like I did, individually frozen for easiest use. They dried fruit if they couldn't eat it all fresh. It was preserved when sugar could be had. It was also made into alcohol.

According to the Oregon Trail Visitor's Center, a common beverage was Vinegar Lemonade:

> **Mix 1 to 2 Tablespoons of Apple Cider Vinegar into a 12 oz. glass of water. Stir in 2 Tablespoons of sugar or to taste, and Drink Up!**

The things I put in my book were ordinary stories of extraordinary people. I am looking forward to writing more about these ordinary women and researching how they were able to carve much out of very little.

The Unspoken Words
By Larry Chura

That will be the day that when you say goodbye..." the old rock-n-roll song came scratchily through the dash speaker of his dad's old truck. Jessie's mind wandered back to when he was a preteen and always seemed to be having "parent trouble." He couldn't count the number of times his dad threatened him with an "attitude adjustment." Fortunately for Jessie, his dad rarely followed through with his threats.

With a sudden pained expression, he remembered the time his dad did erupt and physically threw him across a small rural dirt road into a ditch. He remembered the pain from that day forward and tried to "keep it together."

Jessie also remembered afterwards, when he would accidentally "tick" his dad off, his dad would shake in anger. Surprisingly his dad never threw or hit him again and never mentioned it until the day that he passed.

That day, his dad looked at him with tired and pained eyes as he held Jessie's hand. Starting off with a cough he asked, "Do you remember the throwing incident?"

When he saw Jessie's head nod, he began. "I had never been so mad at you in my whole life, and so sorry afterwards. I tried to never allow my temper to erupt in your direction before and never afterwards. I had a bad temper when I was young and had thought that it was under control. It was that one time that I failed both you and me as a father. I hope that you will forgive me for it because it has been on my mind ever since."

With this, his hand tightened for an instant and then became weak as his head fell back against the pillow. I knew in my heart that he was gone. I cried like a baby realizing that I never told him that I had forgiven him many years ago and now I never could.

Tasting a Memory
By Larry Chura

The warm glass of milk sat on the small kitchen table in front of me. It was the special treat that my Grandma would sometimes make for me on cool afternoons. Special times such as these were rare for us. My Grandma, or "Baba" as she was called by my sister and me, was an only child and, in growing up, she had a stern taskmaster of a father. When she became of age, she was married off to a carbon copy of her dad. It was just how things were done back then. She herself had only one child; a daughter, my mom. The mistrust of all males was very strongly ingrained into her. She tolerated my dad and me simply because we were family. Grandpa had died of a heart attack followed by a stroke some years before when I was 4. She had then fallen back into the habit of taking care of herself and not asking for any help from anyone.

Outside, the weather was changing and the long and hot Canadian plain's summer was transforming into the changes that made it fall. This wasn't the rapid turning of leaf color that happened to the east and the west. It was more the lessening of tornado warnings, thunderstorms and endless days of oppressive dusty heat. These first cool evenings were a treat that called for a sitting down and exhaling from all the 'have-tos' that filled the day.

Grandma was a thin and willowy woman who was far from being weak in any sense. She had hard, piercing blue eyes that would seemingly never show tenderness. It always seemed to me that she was covering all her bases and judging those around her. Her hair was gray-white with age and long, held up with old hair pins in a bun. Her house dress was plain, faded gray with some old embroidered flowers on it. In many ways she looked like she had fallen from the pages of an old western wagon train story. It seemed that those who had gone through the Great Depression, whether they be in Canada or in the States, had the same guardedness about them.

"Well Larry," she began, "what have you done today that you can be proud of and call your own?"

When she had first asked me this type of question I was caught unawares. I didn't know how to answer it. I had never given that line of questioning much thought. I was also scared that I would answer it wrong. It wasn't panic, it was me trying to not get a mental "whiplash" from thinking in opposite directions at the same time. As so many children tend to do, I wanted to please my grandma. For the life of me, I couldn't think of anything that was the "right" answer.

In desperation, I replied, "I tried to have fun in everything that I had to do."

Her reaction surprised me. She leaned back in her chair and smiled at me. Looking back, I can see it as a "grasshopper" moment. At the time, I was totally confused. She got up from her chair and returned with some tea for herself and two cookies. She gave me one and started talking to me. I felt for the first time she was talking to me, not at me.

"Larry," she began, "you have stumbled on a truth that you will need to hang on to for your whole life. That truth is simply this: When you have or want to do anything, try to find some part of it that is fun. Focus on that part and the task will soon be done with little boredom or problems. In fact, the time doing it will seem to fly away. It won't make it less hard or tiresome, because that is part of most things we do. It will give you a leg up on most people that are always complaining about this or that. This truth is sadly something that a person has to discover for themselves to truly appreciate and accept. You have now started the discovery process that will change you into a fun loving 'big person.' If you let yourself grow, your life will be one of discovery mixed in with some joy."

I realized at that moment that I was finally sitting at the "grown up" table. It started for me a life-long path of discovery to find out what were the unspoken "hidden" rules that made the world spin around. My relationship with my maternal grandmother had also changed. I wasn't just a bothersome, albeit cute, boy any more. I was more of an adult in training whose opinions were heard and considered. To this day, when it has been a long hot one in late summer and I have a glass of milk along with a cookie in the evening, I can see my "Baba" sitting at the table and smiling at me. It is truly the tasting of a memory. What can I say, it brings a smile to my face.

Meeting Julie
By Gene Conrad

A few years after I graduated from high school, I was living in Eugene, Oregon, with my roommate, Doug. We were contractors, specializing in building gazebos and decks. We also went to church together and decided to go to a church convention in Boring, Oregon. Yes... that is an actual place.

While we thought these gatherings were interesting, we also enjoyed the social aspects. I had met a cute and friendly young lady named Teresa who was planning on being there, and by my estimate, she seemed to be mildly interested in me... an overestimate on my part, I was to find out.

A few days after the convention ended, Teresa invited Doug and me to come to Portland. She and her sister, Carolee, were planning a get-to-gether on Labor Day weekend for the young people who had attended the meeting. The plan was for all of us to go windsailing at Vancouver Lake north of Portland. Since Eugene is about 120 miles south of Portland, she invited us to stay at their cousin's place along with some of the other guys from out of town... "Just bring a sleeping bag and plan on sleeping on the floor."

This sounded great to us, so we got directions to the "Brouse House," as they called the place. We worked like mad to make sure we could take the time off. There was only a couple of days warning, so we had to hustle.

We were to arrive on Friday at the Brouse House, spend the night and on Saturday we would go to Vancouver Lake for a windsailing lesson before spending the rest of the afternoon cruising the lake. There was also a picnic area that had been reserved with a beach volleyball court. Then, on Saturday evening, everyone would gather at the Brouse House for supper and to sing hymns. The boys would stay the night there and the girls would go to another home for the night. Sunday morning, everyone would meet back at the Brouse House for a morning fellowship meeting and then disperse after that.

The Brouse House was going to be the hub of all of the action, and we would be staying there! Sounded better all the time.

Doug and I left early and made our way through the Portland Labor Day traffic. We found the Brouse House without incident at about 5:30 in the evening. The house was big and friendly-looking, so we parked under the trees, walked to the front door and rang the doorbell.

After a few moments, a woman opened the door with a bit of a quizzical look on her face. Doug and I asked if this was the Brouse House and introduced ourselves. There was another brief pause before she smiled brightly, introduced herself as Jennie and opened the door wide for us.

We came in and immediately felt welcome. Despite the warm day, the house was cool and comfortable. Through French doors to the right of the entry was a room known as the music room, with a piano, couch and chairs. Straight ahead into the family room there was a fireplace with more couches and a window at the back of the house revealing a covered patio with a wicker table, chairs and a grill. The kitchen smelled great and it looked like Jennie was working up a big batch of spaghetti.

"Will there be many other guys staying tonight?" I asked. "We have our sleeping bags with us. Can we bring them in and put them some place out of the way?"

"I'm not sure how many will be coming," Jennie replied with a smile. "But if you would like to bring your things in, you can put them in the Music room. You can all sleep in there on the floor if that's ok."

"Sure!" we said, and went off to bring in our things.

It wasn't until a couple of weeks later that we learned that the Brouse family was aware only of the windsailing weekend, but that was it. They had not been informed that their house would be the hub and there would be several guys crashing there for the weekend. Jennie laughed that she had just happened by chance to make a big pot of spaghetti that evening.

Jennie put Doug and I to work – she is really good at that – putting additional leaves in the table, rounding up chairs and setting the table. The doorbell started ringing fairly frequently. I think there were eventually about a dozen guys that showed up that night for dinner and to stay the weekend.

During the bustle of getting supper on the table, Jennie's husband Dick came home from his medical clinic. Their children, Julie, Dan and Heidi also arrived. They were not super-surprised by the commotion and slipped right into helping out with getting things ready. The Brouse family was very hospitable and we found out later, they were used to entertaining large groups.

After supper, some of us wandered out to the barn to help with chores. The four horses were brought in, fed and watered.

The next morning, we had a great breakfast and started getting ready to head out to the lake. Food was packed and we loaded their car, a Lincoln Mark V. When it was time to go, Jennie handed me the keys and informed me I was driving. I had no idea how to get to where we were headed, so they directed me through Portland traffic to the lake.

The Mark V was probably the nicest car I had driven to that point. The car was packed with several conversations going on at once. I was a little white-knuckled most of that first drive. Portland traffic is much more intense than I was used to, but Jennie would just laugh when I had to stomp on the throttle to work through traffic. Boy, that car could move!

It was a diesel, so the black cloud left behind on acceleration was referred to as "crop dusting" by the family. The only other diesel I had driven was a worn-out Isuzu that sounded like it would rattle apart any moment.. not the case here.

I was also impressed that the car had a cell phone in it. At that time (late 80s) cell phones were rare and definitely not pocket-sized. It consisted of a handset with a curly cord attached to a unit about the size of a breakfast cereal box. All it lacked was a crank on the side and an antenna to stretch up to make it look like those wind-up two-way radios the military uses in the WWII movies.

We arrived at the lake after a drive of about 40 minutes. The group of young people totaled around 45 and everyone was friendly and happy. A busy volleyball game was already in progress and food was piled up on a couple of tables. We ate lunch and then were informed how the afternoon would progress.

We got in line to fill out the paperwork and pay for our lesson and board rental. The lesson was for newbies and would be on dry ground. Several of the kids had boards already, and they hit the lake after lunch. For some reason, I managed to get the last of the rental boards. I was told it was a sport model. The board was smaller than average and the sail bigger than average and was designed for those who wanted to do acrobatic moves. The instructors seemed to be feeling a bit of pressure because the group was bigger than expected, and the breeze was picking up a bit; some cloud cover was also beginning to form.

The boards were spread out on the grass next to the lake for the lesson which consisted of:
1) Make sure your life jacket is properly clipped on; 2) This is how you stand on the board and hold the bar on the sail; 3) End of lesson; and 4) Go sailing.

That seemed pretty easy to me. No problem, right? We all headed for the water, and since I was the last one to get a board, I was also among the last to actually get into the water.

The breeze was picking up significantly and there was a bit of chop forming on the lake. The direction of the wind was blowing from the docks straight across the lake. The cloud cover was also growing, and there was enough to block out the direct sunlight; it was starting to cool off.

One of the instructors helpfully threw my board in the lake and sent me after it. I plunged into the water and made my way to the board. Even though the sail was lying in the water, the chop and the wind was moving it away from the dock. I had to hustle to catch up to it.

Now it was time to hop on and start sailing! Keep in mind that I am about as suited for water sports as a giraffe is for driving a VW Bug. I think

I must have tried to get on that stupid thing at least a hundred times. Most of the time, the waves were enough to dump me back in. If I did manage to stand up, trying to drag that extra big sail out of the water was pretty much impossible. The water was cold and the wind and overcast made it even colder.

After a while, I heard what sounded like an outboard motor. I draped my arms across the board while dangling in the water and looked around. It looked like most of the group was in the same fix, stranded because of the strong wind and choppy water. The outboard motor was on a raft that was going out to each person. They hauled each one into the boat, then had them hold onto the mast of their board while they towed it back to the dock. The boat could only hold three people besides the driver, so it was going to take a while before they got to me.

I noticed that my small board and big sail had worked! I had drifted the farthest across the lake, and was actually starting to enter into a patch of weeds along the far shore... without actually sailing!

The boat was picking up people closest to the dock first and it looked like I would be dead last.

The wind was still bad and the chop showed a bit of foam and white caps. The loaded boat was really struggling to get back to the dock against the wind and current.

I managed to wiggle up out of the water into a sitting position on the board. I pulled my knees up to my chest and wrapped my arms around them to try to stay warm. I shivered uncontrollably as I watched the boat go back and forth bringing in sailors from all over the lake. Now that I was on top of the board, the wind had something bigger to push against and I continued to drift. Yep, I would be last.

They finally picked up the guy closest to me, then motored my way. They stopped about 60 feet away and motioned for me to swim out... against the current, dragging my big-sail board. Oy.

I rolled off of the board into the water and learned why they had stopped so far away. There was only about two feet of water and I sunk in the mud almost to my knees.

I slogged my way through the mud to where the water was deep enough to swim. As I approached the boat, the guy in the boat told me to grab the end of the mast of a board they were dragging. I thought they were going to use that to help me get to the boat. Nope... not the plan. As soon as I had a grip on the very end of the mast, they yelled at me to hang on and gunned the engine.

I was lying on my belly on the board, hanging onto it with one hand while maintaining a death grip on the mast they were dragging me with. Compound that with the cold, the waves, the wind and the wake from the boat, and it was all I could do to hang on. I was gradually being pulled off of my board, and by the time we finally made it to the dock, I was pretty sure I could not held on for another second. I was so happy to be back on solid ground!

We got into dry clothes. I made quite a fashion statement in my shorts and tube socks. (Yes, Dork blood runs pretty thick in my veins.) We warmed up by playing volleyball and eating more food. The weather was not really getting any better, so we decided to pack it up and everyone would head back to the Brouse House for even more food and time together.

I drove the Mark V back and was starting to really like that car. At the house, everyone made themselves comfortable and were conversing in small groups all through the house and out on the patio. I was visiting with Teresa and getting the distinct impression that she was not interested. Toward the end of our conversation, she asked me if I had met her cousin, Julie, and pointed her out across the room.

"No, I haven't." I said.

I had noticed her the evening before, but in all of the commotion we had not really met. She had really pitched in by helping her mom deal with all of the extra company and seemed to be a very capable gal. Gorgeous, too, and that was a plus.

"You should meet her," Teresa said. "I think you would really like her."

About that time it was announced that we could eat again, so we all headed for the kitchen and dug in. I don't know where all that food came from, but there was always plenty. After eating we wandered out to the music room to sing hymns.

I love to sing and there were many excellent singers there. I noticed Julie had an amazing voice so I stayed pretty close and enjoyed hearing her. We started visiting between songs, and continued after the singing ended that evening. The next day after lunch, she told me about her recent trip to the Soviet Union with People to People. She had spent a month there and the trip had left a powerful impression on her. She was definitely leaving an impression on me.

One of the things that came up in conversation was the possibility of getting a group together to see the *Nutcracker.* I didn't really know what that was, some kind of a play or something like that. I said that sounded like fun and Julie said she would start working on finding out who might like to go. I said I would like to go, so she promised to keep me in the loop. I think it was a test.

By the end of the weekend, I was completely smitten. It took a while to get her reeled in, but that will have to be another story...

Reading and Miss Rock

By Dale R. Dickson

I have a great love of literature. The book of life is brief, and I want to read as much as possible. My father taught me to read before I entered first grade, and I soon read all the books within my reading ability in our vast family library.

I was in 3rd grade when we moved to Greenville, Pennsylvania. I soon was introduced to the public library situated in the high school building. One section of it was for school kids, grades 1 through 12, and the other section was for adults only.

Miss Rock was the librarian, towering at not a hair over five feet, and she was very strict when enforcing her rules and restrictions on those of us who utilized the library.

She often visited all the classrooms in our grade school, encouraging us to check out books in the library, and brought some with her in an effort to pique our interest in reading. She definitely had a prejudice in books she obtained for the library. She did not approve books that had violence, exhibits of anger, or things that were not "nice" in the title.

One of my classmates asked her if she had the book *No Safe Place to Hide* in the library. Miss Rock replied, "Oh no! Just the title of the book tells us what the story is about, and I will not allow books such as this one in the library."

At home I told my father what had happened in school that day, and Miss Rock's remark about books. Fortunately dad found the same book in our own library and read some of it with me. It was not at all what Miss Rock had surmised, but a happy story about kids living in a large house and playing with their fun-loving dog.

Dad explained the concept of "judging a book by its cover," and that was what Miss Rock had done. This was a very good lesson for me, and I was to employ it often in my lifetime, both with books and with people.

I wondered how many books she had prevented us from reading.

We could check out only a maximum of three books at a time, and had to keep them for a minimum of two weeks before being able to check out more books. Miss Rock felt no one could read books faster than that. This really hindered my reading, but her rules were the law in the library.

One summer day I checked out my three books and had one of them nearly read before I walked home.

Once there was a summer reading contest where each reader had his name on an image of a paper balloon. When a book was read the balloon was moved higher on a large poster, gradually hoping to reach the moon, the goal of the contest.

Well, my balloon was the first one to reach the moon; there wasn't another balloon close to me.

I often crossed the hall to visit the adult library, browsing through the shelves, but Miss Rock was always there, strictly reminding me I could not check out any book from the adult library.

I did find a book I really wanted to read, but Miss Rock wouldn't let me check it out, even though I asked her nicely.

I mentioned this to my dad, who was a teacher at Greenville High School, and he told me to meet him after school outside the adult library door. This I did, and we entered the library. He told me to pick out the book I wanted and bring it to him. He was reading a newspaper when I approached him with my book.

I followed him to the check-out desk where Miss Rock was sitting. He turned to me and said, "Is this the book you want, Son?"

I replied, "Yes, it is."

He turned to Miss Rock and told her, "Please check this book out for me."

Miss Rock gave me a very unlady-like look, obviously realizing what was happening. But she checked out the book in dad's name, and he gave it to me.

I never used my dad to get books for me in this manner again, but I am certain Miss Rock didn't forget how a schoolboy and his dad duped her.

Just another page from the book of life.

....

World War II Is Ended!
By Dale R. Dickson

I remember when World War II was over. I was eight years old. We heard the welcomed news on the radio, and the small village of Sheakleyville, Pennsylvania went wild in celebration. All the church bells were ringing, and people were outside their houses, laughing, crying and hugging each other. My older brother Deem and I tied some cans on a string and fastened them to the rear of our bicycle. He pedaled the bike, with me sitting on the handlebars, trying to make as much celebrating noise as possible, dragging the cans behind us.

Two days later, a drum and bugle corps from Camp Reynolds Army Base in nearby Greenville made a visit to our town. They started from the cemetery on the north side of town, and after a brief celebration honoring the fallen military men from the area, began the one-mile march down Route 19 to the fairgrounds at the schoolyard.

A troop of boys my age followed along, marching in unison. All of us had small plastic horns, and we played them to accompany the buglers. We really enjoyed imitating the buglers when they were marching between musical pieces, and held their bugles with the bell positioned against their thigh, and the mouthpiece placed horizontally to their side.

This especially pleased us when onlookers applauded us for our attempts to imitate the buglers.

To cap off the day's celebration, one of the soldiers ran full speed and dived through the air, and flew head-first through the bass drum and deftly made a flip once he was through the drum and landed on his back, continuing on a roll until he rose to his feet. Now, that was one thing none of us wanted to try!

Another way of celebrating was soon experiencing the end of food stamps, rationing gasoline and rubber tires. There wouldn't be any more black-outs and air raid alerts. We did continue working our many victory gardens, though. That was a task the whole family enjoyed.

Photo Gallery

Groundwaters' own Pat Broome at the age of 10.

Pat Broome lives with her husband Dennis and son Jonathan in Veneta, Oregon. She is a retired library cataloger and a Women's Army Corps (WAC) veteran. Pat and Dennis were assigned to duties in Germany and lived in Europe for 5 years. While living there in 1981, Pat traveled to the Soviet Union. After their return to the U.S., Pat eventually obtained a Master of Arts degree in History. Once in Oregon, she became a volunteer and member of the Fern Ridge Library Board of Directors in Veneta. She also became part of the *Groundwaters* family from the its beginnings as a copy editor and sometime contributor. Pat and Dennis now volunteer in the summer as Park Hosts with the Oregon State Parks System on the Oregon Coast, accompanied by one of their two Beagles (Ruby, the Quiet One). The other Beagle (Charlie, the Noisy One) stays behind with their son, Jonathan. Some of her interests are: European and American History, Holocaust Studies, historical mysteries, dogs and Star Trek.

The Quest for Happy Endings
By Pat Edwards

Her name was Ruth Smith, but I came to know her as "Dolly," as many others did. She entered my life in June 2011, when she first submitted a story called "Tuscaloosa, Alabama; I Was There" to *Groundwaters* magazine. I was managing editor of the literary quarterly which we distributed free to libraries, senior centers, businesses and organizations throughout Lane County, Oregon. Dolly had picked up a copy at the Junction City Library near the retirement residence where she lived. Her story told of her college years in Tuscaloosa during World War II. It had been triggered by the news of the devastating 2011 tornado season that hit Tuscaloosa rather hard that year and it brought forth some poignant memories which she shared with our readers.

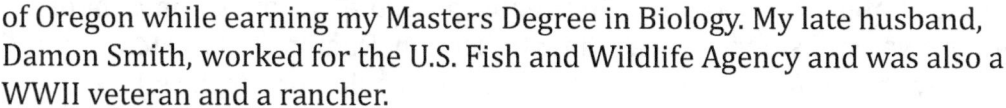

In her 2011 bio, Dolly told a little about her life:

"I was a biology major at UCLA after leaving the University of Alabama. I then worked as an instructor and histologist at the University of Oregon while earning my Masters Degree in Biology. My late husband, Damon Smith, worked for the U.S. Fish and Wildlife Agency and was also a WWII veteran and a rancher.

"Damon and our daughter, Judy, are both gone now and I moved to a retirement residence in Junction City three years ago to be with other people. I was overjoyed when I found a copy of *Groundwaters* a couple of years ago. It is an excellent magazine. Thank you for your efforts and good works."

After that, the mail began to bring other submissions on a regular basis– mainly poetry that Dolly had written, and one day we received the first of several donation checks she sent us, tucked neatly inside a letter containing her most recent poem.

Upon finding out that she was living in a senior residence, I began hand-delivering copies of Groundwaters to her when I did my distribution run to the Junction City Library. Her home was only a few blocks out of the way and when I knocked and stuck my head in the open door that first time, she greeted me with a smile. When I told her who I was, she worked her way to her feet using her walker and threw out her arms to demand a hug in greeting. Her excitement in meeting me was spontaneous and humbling. I sat and visited with her for a short time during which she showed me her desk and the journal that she wrote in as often as she could when her health would allow. It wasn't long before I had to head out to make my other deliveries, but I knew that I'd be back when it was time to distribute the next issue.

On later visits, Dolly told me about her love of her homeplace which she still owned. It was part of a ranch on Grimes Road that her husband's grandparents,William A. and Eliza Jane Smelser Smith, had homesteaded in the late 1800s. Because of my love for the history of our local area, I was eager to learn more about her past, but I missed the chance to learn more directly from Dolly. Her close friend, Anne Maggs-Foster, however, was able to supply some of the details of Damon and Dolly's very interesting life.

"I met Damon and Ruth in 1982 when we purchased 28 acres from them. Our acreage was 3 of 10 strips of land that fell across both sides of the little valley where their homeplace is now.

"His grandfather homesteaded 160 acres of the valley when he rode out to Oregon on a saddle horse. The main valley is the one Ferguson runs through and the old, original Smith homestead was on a small knoll to the north and east of the current intersection of Ferguson and Grimes Roads. The stage coach used to run along the top of the ridge because the bottom land would flood.

"Grimes Road used to be a wooden road which made it passable in the winter. When we first moved out there, the old, one-room school house was still standing near the intersection. Damon said the teacher lived with them (which he hated because he could not cut class!)

"Damon told us that his dad, Walter Leston Smith, was one of ten kids. When the kids were grown, Damon's grandfather, William A. Smith, split the side valley along Grimes Road into ten, 10-acre, strips and gave one to each of their children. Damon's dad slowly collected all of the strips as his siblings either moved away or died off, and Damon inherited the majority of the original homestead.

"Damon's mother, Callie Lilly Wolf, grew violets and she used to trade varieties with old man Kneibl who lived on Ferguson Road. The Smith's old abandoned homeplace was on our piece of land, as were the big barns and many small outbuildings.

"Ruth met Damon when she was looking for a squirrel skeleton for a biology class at the University of Oregon. He was a "cowboy" and she fell for him. They used to have horses and we rode with the both of them for many a mile on the logging roads up behind our place. She told me that they built the house with hand tools – no electricity at the time. They had an outdoor privy until her mom came to visit after Damon and Ruth's daughter, Judy, was born, and said that, with a baby to take care of, she needed an inside bathroom.

"Ruth was highly skilled in methods of canning and cooking. She processed and preserved whatever Damon hunted. I think her story about a woman named "Zoe" was modeled on herself as a capable, homesteader. Ruth could shoot and cook, care for her family and home, be a good neighbor and a 'second' grandma to my kids, and keep a positive outlook on life.

"She gained her teaching credential by correspondence and taught school at Junction City High School after Judy was born. She taught art and science and, for many years displayed the pictures her students had painted.

"In the early 90s, we gave Ruth our old Macintosh computer when we upgraded our home computer. My daughter, Amity, and I taught her how to use it and she began writing in earnest. She would write on a yellow pad, then transcribe it into the computer where she could edit with ease. When the old timers came to visit Damon – and there was a steady stream of men – she questioned them about wildlife and plants and stories of how things were done so that she could infuse her writing with the lore of the times she was writing about.

"Ruth was a unique person who loved life and lived it fully."

Dolly Ruth Smith, as she liked her byline to read, was indeed a unique and wonderful woman who managed to wend her way into my heart as our much-too-short friendship evolved. I didn't get to see her often, but when I did, she was always so excited to see me. Sometimes, she had a friend visiting who she would introduce me to as "her editor." Other times, I would find her confined to bed following what she called "small stokes." In about 2013, I learned that she had fallen and injured her leg. I traveled to Junction City to visit her in the rehab center next to her assisted living apartment, but when I arrived, I was told that she had been taken to one in Eugene, instead. So, I tracked her down there. When she saw me enter the room, her face lit up and it warmed my heart. After several more weeks, she was transferred back to her apartment in Junction City.

Dolly began an obvious decline at that point, but whenever I visited, she'd talk about the new story that she was writing... a fairytale. As time went on, it seemed to grow in importance to her, even though her ability to work on the story was hindered by failing health. She said that she'd dream about the story and would try to get it on paper the next day, since she was no longer using a computer, but it was not coming together as well as she wanted. She was especially obsessed with the ending that was just not working out for her.

By October 2014, she decided that the story which she titled "Angela" was going to have to be good enough, although, obviously, she still was not happy with it. She had her niece, Martha Mattus, type it for her and she sent it to *Groundwaters* as a submission for our January 2015 issue.

I was a bit surprised by the story when we received it. It was not her normal style of writing and it was written with an almost child-like imagination, but I personally knew how much it meant to Dolly, so I promised her that we would use it in January. I also promised that I'd help her figure out an ending for it. Before I could prepare the story for publication, however, I received an email from Martha, who lived in Portland. She said that Dolly was once again in rehab – this time in Junction City – and that she was not expected to live more than a week or two. Dolly asked her to notify her friends and if we wanted to say a last goodbye, we should do so right away.

When I got there, Dolly, herself, told me that she didn't expect to see her story in print. I assured her that it would be in the January issue and I'd be bringing it to her as I always did. I added an "ending" to it that would reflect her passing and brought her a mock-print of the story as it would look in *Groundwaters*. It seemed strange at the time because I was talking about her passing, but Dolly seemed touched by it.

Amazingly, Dolly rallied in late December... at least it would have been amazing for someone else, but Dolly had grit and I believe that she somehow willed herself better. I changed the ending again, which still was not satisfactory, but I was able to deliver that January issue to Dolly in person... but she still was not happy with the story.

"Angela" once again became a passion for her as she lay in one rehab center bed after another. Months passed, and each time I would visit, she would hold up her yellow writing pad to show me that she was still working on her story. She was determined to get it right, despite her increasingly failing health.

In May 2015, she began slipping into what seemed to be semi-conscious, coma-like states, but she then amazed her caretakers by rousing enough to eat her meals and talk a bit.

On May 13, I went to see her. She was barely responsive. When entered her room, she stirred and opened her eyes, but didn't speak or show recognition. I took her hand and told her who I was, but she didn't seem to understand. Before I left, a nurse came in to take her temperature and gave her a kiss on the cheek. She talked quietly to her and Dolly smiled a couple of times. She seemed to respond when I mentioned to the nurse that those hands she was holding had written some beautiful poetry and stories... and she smiled. As I was leaving, I leaned over and gave her a kiss on the cheek to tell her goodbye, I told her that I would make sure that Angela would live happily ever after. With eyes still closed, she formed the words "Thank you" and smiled.

Dolly was put under hospice care shortly afterwards and peacefully passed away in her sleep on Tuesday, July 22, 2015.

By then I knew that in her mind, Dolly was Angela, and this amazing, wonderful lady had written her own happy ending.

ADDENDUM...

My hope was to reprint Dolly's story of Angela using the revisions that she labored over during her final months. But, the ravages of age and illness had taken their toll on her writing.

Despite that, Angela's story unfolded to reveal her discovery that Donny was shallow and irresponsible and as time passed, Angela found her true love in the person of strong and handsome Alex.

Ruth died knowing that Angela would indeed live happily ever after with her soulmate and eternal love.

She had found not only Angela's happy ending,
but her own, as well.

Rest in Peace, Sweet Lady!

Mister Muffett
By David R.L. Erickson

Mister Jimmy Muffett just showed up one day. It wasn't a particularly eventful occasion and where he came from is fodder, perhaps, for idle speculation on a rainy day. Nevertheless, one bright morning recorded nowhere in anyone's journal, he wandered in on little cat feet and decided to stay. As many cats are likely to do, he chose us, not the other way around. He was traveling light: no identification, no baggage, no apparent attachments, just a gangly bag of bones in a scruffy old tuxedo. The girls, tenured and aloof, tested him briefly for compatibility on the periphery of their loosely-structured sorority and worthiness to share their habitat. His polite manner and lack of swagger won them over.

TigerLily, stalwart stalker of small rodents and nobody's sweetheart, clarified for him certain boundaries, like the ownership of her food bowl and the contents therein. Sedona, Mistress of the Realm, immediately deemed him inconsequential. Muffett, as we called him then (partly because we weren't sure at first what his gender was and, later, because two syllables roll off the tongue more smoothly than six), became the alpha eunuch without a drop of blood being shed. The position had been open for years and no serious applications had been received prior to his arrival.

Oh, later there was blood, to be sure, as neighborhood toms would stroll onto the property on occasion; some just passin' through, others looking for something more specific like untended food or casual companionship. Our adopted boy may not have always won these exchanges, tail-up posturings and yowled warnings followed by tooth and claw, but he obviously gave as good as he got. Eunuch or no, he'd learned to scrap long before his advent among us and the uninvited learned to keep a discrete distance.

His attire, that frazzled tux, was a luxurious, silken pelt at the follicle level, but for some reason known only to the God of Cats, his fur would twine upon itself and mat up so swiftly you could almost watch it happening as he lay curled in blissful repose. In the wintertime, if some cursory grooming was not enacted with regularity, the fur on his neck, belly and skirt would resemble the tread of an off-road tire, which made subsequent grooming an unpleasant experience for all concerned. Eventually, though, my darling Christina would ply him with tasty morsels and he would submit with an un-catlike degree of patience as she sheared, shaved and sawed through clumps and knobs of hair with a texture approaching that of cartilage. When he finally had enough and was given his leave, he looked as though he'd been groomed with a cheese grater. In warmer weather he tolerated a military crew cut from mane to the root of his tail (its bad form to shave a fellow's tail, you know) and, we liked to imagine, he was happier for it.

Muffett wasn't a skittish fellow. Never one for darting about, his preferred locomotive modus was the amble, the deliberate and stately mosey. I saw him run once. I don't believe he considered it worth the effort.

With the girls, he was satisfied being an outdoor cat and, like them, privileged to overnight in the garage where food, water, a clean catbox and soft accommodations were always available, as was heat from a small wood stove in cold weather. Lately though, he asked to come inside off and on during the daytime. He liked our company and, because he was amiable and well-mannered, we allowed him a greater degree of autonomy. As hot weather descended upon us, the house was cool and, when the front door was open, he learned to open the screen door himself, ingress and egress at his discretion. He made one of the bar stools at the island counter his own and we let him have it. No one else was using it.

When we saw that Muffett wouldn't or couldn't eat the standard-issue dry food anymore, we made a special soft blend for him. He didn't eat much and he seemed to be sleeping more than usual. He had a shady haven underneath the tomato plants in the garden he liked during the day, but his favorite, oddly enough, was a spot atop the island counter between the wicker basket of accumulated this 'n' that and a shifting stack of unclassified mail. When I first observed this , I thought it inadvisable to promote such behavior, even though we don't prepare food in that area. I castigated him harshly, shooed him away and sent him outside with prejudice. The next time I hauled him up by the scruff and plopped him down at the door with a strident disclaimer. Instead of pushing aside the screen door and marching away with a haughty tail in the air, he fell over. That I did not expect. In my humble experience cats rarely fall over. I understood at that disheartening moment how fragile he'd become and was disappointed in myself for not recognizing it sooner.

My far-more-sensitive and tender distaff partner gently observed that Muffett was much older than we thought, older than he's acted since adopting us. He'll be leaving us soon, she assured me. More than anything, she said, he just wants to be near us now because now is all he knows. We love him up and tend his matted hair and let him sleep where he's comfortable and we feed him. If someone else was going to give him all that, he'd be there instead, wouldn't he? So we agreed that as long as he didn't migrate to the food-prep territories and remained continent, we'd allow our fading old boy an exclusive, non-transferable countertop dispensation. And so it came to pass.

This morning, he couldn't get up onto his personal barstool. He tried and fell. He wouldn't eat. He went into the bathroom and curled up in a ball behind the toilet. Christina held him, warmed him, talked to him in sweet tones. He couldn't even manage a purr. When she put him down, he hid behind the toilet again.

The vet was in. Muffett cried a little in his carrier on the ride there. He's never been fond of confinement, but he was calm when I took him out in the procedure room. I was very gentle and told him we wouldn't be there very long. He didn't struggle as I laid him on his side. I rubbed him with a thumb on his little round forehead and under his ears, the way he likes it, and the vet slipped a needle into a vein in his hind leg. He didn't even flinch. I put my face next to his to tell him he was a Good Boy. I smelled a sharp chemical tang on his breath. One front paw was in my hand. I felt a pulse. And then I didn't.

Nothing left but paperwork and a tiny bag of bones in a scruffy old tuxedo.

Let us not debate whether animals feel love, or have souls, or go to "heaven," wherever that is. Instead, we will spread tobacco and corn meal and we will burn sweetgrass and sage and we will offer a sweet, gentle little spirit our gratitude for time spent and affection shared.

What else matters?

Photo Gallery

My grandmother, Ethel Cuthbertson, was the eldest of three children. She was born in Edinburgh, Scotland, grew up in Oxford, and graduated from one of the Oxford women's colleges in the days before women could get degrees from the University itself. She married an Oxford University lecturer and Fellow of one of the colleges. *Photo shared by author, Carola Dunn*

Carola Dunn is the author of the Daisy Dalrymple mysteries, the Cornish Mysteries, and over 30 Regencies. Born and raised in England, the author now lives with her dog in Eugene, Oregon, USA. http://caroladunn.weebly.com/

The Legend of The White Buffalo Woman
The Basis of Sioux Beliefs
An excerpt from *Wakanisha Is Love Enough*
By Michael Foster

"About two thousand winters ago, Wakan Tanka sent her from the stars. She came to many tribes but they called her by a different name.

There was a time of great famine. Two young Sioux warriors were hunting, trying to find food for their hungry tribe. They found nothing and they were very discouraged. Then, in the distance, they saw a figure walking toward them across the plains. When the figure came close, the two braves could see that it was a beautiful maiden walking barefoot, dressed in pure white buckskin. Her buckskin was so white; she seemed to glow like the sun. Her dress was decorated with sacred symbols so finely done in beadwork, it seemed impossible any woman could do work so fine.

These two braves had never seen a woman so beautiful. Her hair was long and blue black, like liquid stone, tied with a single strand of buffalo hide. Her eyes were filled with intelligence and holy light. Her shape was of the perfect woman, a man's every desire. One of the braves was filled with lust to lie with her in the tall prairie grass.

The other brave said, "This woman is sacred. She may be a vision. You must not try to touch her like an immoral woman."

The first warrior, filled with lust, touched the woman where husbands touch their wives in love. Immediately, a black cloud covered the warrior. Lightning struck him and snakes ate his flesh. When the cloud left, his bones fell black on the prairie.

The second brave fell to his knees, cast his eyes to the ground and prayed to Wakan Tanka.

The woman reached out her hand, lifted the man's head so he could look into her eyes and she said, "A man who looks first to a woman's outer beauty will never know her divine beauty for there is dust upon his eyes and he is blind. But a man who sees in a woman the spirit of the Great One and sees her beauty first in spirit and truth, that man will know God in that woman."

The man's eyes filled with tears for love of this woman. She said, "Have no fear, you too shall have what you desire. You and your friend symbolize the two paths that men can If first you seek the Great Spirit, you will find what you need from the earth; it will come readily into your hands. But if you first seek to secure your earthly desires and forget the spirit, you will inside."

Then the young hunter asked who she was. Her gaze pierced him to his soul and she said, "I am the Spirit of Truth and the face of the Great Spirit your people have forgotten. Tell your chief to prepare a tipi tonight that I may come to your people to teach them sacred things that once they knew but no longer remember."

The brave returned to his people and told the chief what had happened. The chief ordered a great lodge built hoping they would receive teaching from one who lived among the stars.

That night she came to their camp. Without speaking, she walked around the central fire seven times in the direction the sun travels across the sky. Each time her feet touched the sand all those there felt her reverence for the Earth. Few dared look into her eyes but those who did saw into the universe and felt naked and revealed, like who they truly were. Her voice was like water in a stream or of birds singing love.

"Seven times I have circled this fire in silence and reverence." she said. "This fire is like the love that burns forever in the heart of the Great Spirit. It is the same fire that warms the heart of every buffalo, every eagle, every rabbit and every human. The spirit of Wakan Tanka is in all things."

She stopped and looked at each person there. Then she continued, "This fire that burns at your center is your love and it is right at times to express this love sexually. This passion, if you do not control it, is like a wildfire that will destroy everything. But with wisdom, this passion will create many generations and warm thousands of lodges through hundreds of snowy winters. With reverence, this passion will give its power to your children's children's children."

She looked at each person again and said, "Remember the brave whose black bones lie in the moonlight. He thought first to show this fire in sex only without thought to the spirit behind it. His way leads to a cycle of illusion and suffering. To follow his way is to weaken your vitality and power."

"Always remember this," she said, "the creative force between a man and a woman is a circle, a sacred hoop. With wisdom and reverence, you gather the power of love in this circle until it explodes outward in new generations. Wakanisha is important in all things!"

She then pulled a burning branch from the fire. "Your people have forgotten the most precious thing, your connection to the Great Spirit. I have come with a fire from heaven to kindle again your memory of what has been and to strengthen you for the times to come."

From a pouch at her side, she took a pipe. The bowl was of red stone and the stem of fine wood. She said, "This sacred pipe represents many things. The bowl is of stone and the stem is from a plant to remind us of the sacredness of the Earth and all living things. The bowl is round and is the symbol of the Sacred Hoop, the cycles of giving and receiving, of breathing out and breathing in, of living and dying."

She held the pipe aloft and addressed the people, "This pipe will help you remember that every breath you take is sacred. Your life is lit from that same fire that burns in the heart of the Great Spirit. Your flame, your individual human life, can light a greater fire ... the flame of love in another's heart and so bring consciousness to the Earth. Keep not the love that burns within you turned towards yourself and your desires but give away that fire that it may burn bright in the helping of each other."

She filled the bowl with the finest herbs, lit it and passed it around the fire seven times. She then taught the People the seven sacred ceremonies.

"The first" she taught them, "is the Keeping of the Soul. At death, they must be purified so they can be reunited with the Great Spirit."

"The second is the Rite of Purification. This must be done in a sweat lodge before any significant undertaking to clean the mind and the spirit."

"The third is Crying for a Vision. You must isolate yourself away from the People and wait for a vision. This vision will help you understand your place in the world."

"The fourth is the Sun Dance. It must be done in the summer on a day with a full moon. You must dance long until you feel the pain of life and the sun's power to renew."

"The fifth is the Making of Relatives. Families come not just by birth or marriage. This ceremony can bring peace between you and another by making you family."

"The sixth is Coming of Age. When a girl first bleeds and then can have children, she must be purified enough to realize that what is happening to her is a sacred thing, becoming a woman."

"The seventh is The Throwing of the Ball. This game represents the course of a person's life and their search for Wakan Tanka. The ball is thrown to the entire tribe only five times during the game, once from each sacred direction and once high into the air to signify as enlightenment coming directly from The Great Spirit. Very few in the tribe will get the ball as very few will experience the Great Mystery. Ignorance makes it nearly impossible to know Wakan Tanka, just as the odds of getting the ball are against you."

After four days of teaching, White Buffalo Woman told the People, "I am leaving but I will return. When I leave, you will see me change four times into four colors. The four colors represent the four colors of men. When you see me return, I will be white and you will know the time of great trouble between men will end.

Then, White Buffalo Woman walked off into the setting sun. The People watched. She lay down on the prairie and rolled and appeared as a black buffalo. The black buffalo then rolled and became a yellow buffalo. She rolled again and became a red buffalo and on the last roll, she became a white buffalo, as white and beautiful as the sun.

To this day, we pray the White Buffalo returns to end these troubles between men."

Lochsa River Rescue

By Dana Graves

I have worked for I.T.D. (Idaho Transportation Department) for nearly seven years. As part of my duties, I help to maintain the highway in one of the most hazardous regions in Idaho, the area between Kooskia (Milepost 75.5) over Lolo Pass to the Montana border near Missoula, Montana (Milepost 174.4) on U.S. Highway 12. I operate a snowplow from late fall to early spring. This is an account of my recollections about an event that took place requiring the rescue of a woman on U.S. Highway 12 who was trapped in an upside down vehicle in the Lochsa River after going over a steep embankment on November 25, 2014.

The day started out with a trip to Fleming from Kooskia to clear numerous rocks on U.S. Highway 12, as it was raining at the lower end. Henry Bailey and I plowed from Fleming Milepost 98 to Milepost 124.8 when we came upon a 2014 Freightliner that was disabled in the westbound lane because of a damaged air tank from hitting a rock. After getting flares out and information from the driver, I called this in to State Com. Then Forest Auto from Lewiston was dispatched. Earlier, a call from Fish Creek call box by a motorist had alerted a service mechanic in Grangeville to head upriver. The weather had turned to heavy rain at the disabled truck, but there was snow up above, so I sent Henry up to help the guys there, while I stayed with the truck to gather additional information for State Com.

After putting an incident and SLOW paddle sign out for traffic, eastbound and westbound, I decided I'd better make a rock run at least to Fish Creek to avoid another incident. The disabled truck was on a straight stretch with flashers on and motorists had plenty of pre-warning that it was there. On my return to the truck, I observed that traffic had no problem safely getting around it in both the eastbound and westbound lanes. I made a decision to make a rock run up to Saddle Camp, Milepost 139, to bump rocks and plow slush on the way up and back to the disabled Freightliner at Milepost 124.8. The service mechanic arrived and replaced an air fitting on the air tank, but the tank had a hole punched in it. The mechanic then headed back downriver to Grangeville. The next call that came from the call box at Fish Creek was the news that the wrecker from Forest Auto had ruined a tire and a rim at Milepost 119 after hitting a rock and needed assistance. A short time later, State Com informed us that Bruneel Tire was enroute from Lewiston with a rim and tire for the wrecker. The ETA (estimated time of arrival) was three hours. A Buell truck was on standby for replacement of the disabled Freightliner. We were just waiting for the wrecker to arrive to take the refrigerated portion of the truck that contained expensive frozen seafood to its destination.

Around 3 o'clock, Henry returned after plowing upriver. It wasn't very long after this that we received the news about a plow truck at Powell which had a disabling hydraulic leak. My foreman, Mark Schuster, sent me upriver to switch out trucks, while Henry stayed with the disabled Freightliner.

At approximately Milepost 151 near the Jerry Johnson Hotsprings, I started plowing snow, as it was accumulating. I plowed center to Powell and switched trucks and plowed centerline down to Milepost 155.5 where a motorist waved me down to inform me of a vehicle in the river. I could see the tail lights. This was about 5:35 in the evening and it was dark. I parked the snowplow in a nearby turnout and instructed a couple of motorists to move their vehicles into the turnout to prevent the possibility of another accident. The snowplow and other vehicles were parked in such a way that they provided some diffused light in the general area but not on the vehicle itself which was much lower in the river.

I set out the first set of flares. After I walked downriver to set out the second set of flares, I yelled down to the vehicle in the river, "Are there any injuries?" and the response was "A minor head injury."

I called State Com and informed them of a vehicle upside down in the river and a passenger with a head injury and also that Ed Holbert ISP (Idaho State Police), had left the scene of the disabled Freightliner at Milepost 124.8 and was headed upriver and would be arriving sometime soon at my location. I also informed State Com that I would be getting back to them soon with some additional information about the people and the vehicle involved.

After surveying the terrain, I decided that spiked caulk or "cork," boots would be needed. I returned to the snowplow to exchange my running shoes for my boots. This particular morning, I had forgotten my regular work boots, and had on my running shoes. How strange and how fortunate! When loading up my gear to head upriver for work, I found my insulated caulk "cork" boots that I had left by accident in my vehicle from the night before. I grabbed them and headed upriver in the snowplow, not having much confidence in the running shoes or the weather. Those spiked boots provided excellent traction as I headed over the bank from the highway to learn more about the situation in the river. As I approached the vehicle which had settled about 15 feet into the river from the bank, I was informed by a young woman from Lapwai that someone was trapped inside the vehicle and she didn't have the strength to get the person out. My cork boots would be an absolute necessity if I were to have a chance to bring her up the embankment IF I could get her out of the confinement of the vehicle. The Lapwai woman's husband had also been trying to help, but was unable to get through the small opening provided.

During the process of assessing the situation inside the wreckage through the upside down driver's side window and through the back door to see what space I had to work with, I found myself entangled in something. My reflective vest, my baseball cap and glasses were in the way, and most irritating, the hand-held radio on my hip was in the river more than once, while the mike stayed attached to my chest. I walked back to shore, laid my glasses and radio inside my baseball cap and took off the orange reflective vest and my personal vest to eliminate the distraction it caused and to make myself more compact so I might have better success in the rescue.

The top of the vehicle, which was a Chevy Tahoe, was embedded around the large boulder with the back pointed upriver, the tail end up in the air and the front end pointing downriver and partially under the water. Only half the width of the window was accessible, due to the collapsed top. The lady was lying trapped in a pool-like area in the front portion of the vehicle (which was actually the roof of the vehicle). The river contained bits of ice and this water was continually running through the vehicle. The crushed top created a hump between the driver's seat and the passenger seat, which meant she had to be pulled from the partially submerged front area over the hump and out the driver's side window. The lights were on and the power switch of the seat could be activated, but the back of the seat only moved about two inches before coming to a stop, due to the crushed top, which was resting against the headrests on the back of the seat. Therefore, I was unable to make any more room in which to work. I found it impossible to pull her to the back opening which had more room, because there definitely was not enough space to move her between the two front seats, so I was forced to work over the hump and within the confined space that this and the crushed driver's window provided.

As I questioned her about her injuries, I determined her main complaints were about having no feeling from the waist down, most likely due to the icy, cold river water in which she was lying. She also asked me not to pull on her left arm; it might come out of the socket. I assumed it was from a previous injury. I discovered she had a heavy leather belt around her waist, so I told her I would try to pull her by her belt.

On the first attempt to pull, she let me know that something was wrong. I was briefly startled in thinking that her feet and legs may be stuck under some metal parts of the wreckage. After closer examination, I discovered that her legs were bent and pinning her as I pulled. I crawled over the top of her to reposition her legs, pointing them down and out through the passenger window toward the river. At this time I got on my belly and moved to halfway in and halfway out the driver's window with my feet sticking out. She became stuck on the lid of a plastic compartment on the ceiling, which was now the bottom/floor, so I ripped it off and threw it out of the way. The trouble was in trying to pull her up over the incline – the hump made by the crushed top. Only then could I finally move her, using the belt around her waist to pull her head first toward the opposite window on the driver's side, even though it was only a few inches at a time. As I was able to escape and was standing in the river, I started the downward pull, which made it much easier. I had the help of the man from Lapwai at this time. I coaxed her to walk, as we held her up by her belt to make it easier to get through the icy cold water, and over large rocks, and finally a few steps through the grass on shore.

It was at that point that she said she was out of energy and collapsed. I remembered my cork boots with the exceptional traction. I told her she could get on my back and put her arms around my neck, piggyback style, and I would take her up the bank on all fours, but she didn't have the strength to hold on.

I then told the man from Lapwai that we needed to put her on her back and skid her up the bank on the snow in the long winter coat that she was wearing. At about the same time that we had decided this was the only way we could get her up the bank and onto the highway, I noticed a tow strap on the steep bank within my reach. It was then that I realized we had help from above, so I tied the strap around my waist and proceeded to pull on her belt, climbing a foot at a time while the man from Lapwai helped by pushing as best he could from below.

The people on the highway at the end of the tow strap were very important to the success in getting the woman up the steep bank. They anchored me to the steep hillside and secured me, as I slowly, step by step, managed to move. This enabled me to pull her up the steep, snow-covered embankment.

When we had finally skidded her (like a sled) and reached the level ground of the highway, I dropped to the ground in the snow, exhausted, trying to catch my breath. I looked down and saw her lying nearby with her hands in the snow. I picked them up and tried to warm them up. They were icy cold. When I was able to talk, I told her she was going to be all right.

I then yelled to everyone around me, "Hey everyone, grab hold, let's load her up and get her warmed up."

A motorist with a Blazer, I believe, had a bed made up in the back and we loaded her into the side back passenger door and cranked up the heater. The people on site offered clothes, sleeping bags, blankets or whatever they had that might be needed.

After everyone involved was inside their own vehicles, warming up, I noticed Idaho State Police Officer Ed Holbert was on the scene. I described the situation to him so he could start the process of sorting it all out. As he took over, it was determined that he didn't need my help. I left the scene with the heater cranked up to high to try to warm up and partially dry off on the trip back downriver to Kooskia.

I did not learn the names of the accident victims and, to my regret, do not know the names of the Lapwai couple who deserved much of the credit.

The number of people who helped in one way or another with this rescue and the importance of the part they played and my admiration for them is hard for me to put into words.

At 4:30, the end of my normal ten-hour work shift, after leaving the disabled truck at Milepost 124.8 and enroute to Powell, I had called State Com and went into extended service (in order to extend my working hours).

I arrived in Kooskia at 8 in the evening and my day had finally come to an end after 14 hours on the job. I parked the truck without refueling or putting my time in the computer, and headed for my home in Stites to warm up, get a hot meal and a warm bed.

This event happened two days before Thanksgiving and it was the BEST Thanksgiving I ever had. I'm sure that, for the woman rescued and the other passengers who had gotten out on their own, it was the best Thanksgiving of their lives, too. We had much to be thankful for!

Photo Gallery

Homesteading Alaska, 1956

Eva, Richard and Royce Newton at Eva's homestead camp in Alaska. (see the following story)

Photos shared by Mildred Thacker Graves

Royce Newton, Joe Seeholzer and Richard Newton at Eva's camp

Homesteading... Alaska Earthquake, 1964
By Mildred Thacker Graves

In 1956, Eva Newton, my sister's mother-in-law, left Oregon and headed for Alaska where her three sons were living. Shortly after arriving, she filed a claim under the Homestead Act on 160 acres of land 40 miles by air and 70 miles by water from Anchorage, Alaska, on the Big Suistna River. Hers was the first homestead in the area. The requirements under the Homestead Act was to build a cabin, toilet facilities and garbage disposal, clear 20 acres of land and spend 5 months a year for 5 years on the homestead.

In the summer of 1956 she bought an old house, tore it down and used some of the material (which had to come by boat) to build a 12 x 14 foot one-room cabin. She camped out in bear country while it was being built with some help from her three sons, Charles, Royce and Richard, who lived in Anchorage. In the summers she spent time clearing her land. It took 3 trees per day to heat her cabin. She also planted a garden each summer. She spent two to six months at a time without leaving. Staples were flown in and she hunted for caribou, fox, and moose and fished for salmon. Later her daughter, Grace Newton Lydic Seeholzer, and her husband, Joe, filed a claim near Eva and began the process of trying to complete all the requirements of obtaining land under the Homestead Act.

By 1964, Grace and Joe Seeholzer were on their homestead in Suisitna Station, Alaska, and Grace's son, Bill Lydic and his wife, Audie and their children, Randy and Laciene had claimed a homestead of their own as well. It was very unusual for all 3 generations to be homesteading at the same time and in the same area.

On March 27, 1964, an earthquake hit, but fortunately Grace's mother, Eva Newton, was not on her homestead at the time.

Grace wrote a letter of the account to family members. Her letter was to be forwarded on to friends in the manner of a chain letter. When my mother, Laura Thacker, received the letter, she hand-copied it before forwarding it to the next name on the list of proposed recipients. The letter was misplaced for a number of years, and upon discovering it and re-reading it, we were again struck by Grace's vivid description of the event and felt that it should be shared. (Please note: In the letter, Grace writes as Nick Barbul, a native who had a homestead near them, speaks. The dog food preparation she writes about was to feed their dog team.) The letter follows as written:

Grace Seeholzer's Letter – Her Experience of the Earthquake of March 27, 1964 at Anchorage, Alaska:

My Dearest Mother, Sisters & Families:

Once again God has been good to us and spared our loved ones in this terrible disaster, for which we have been thankful in prayer.

Joe & I were convinced for a time our number was up. We were each outside clinging to a tree while our whole world was twisting and writhing, as if in agony and a rumbling of drums seemed to be heralding all the demons of hell to join in their devil dance.

Never did a tree seem so wonderful, as I clung to that old spruce. It was the only solid thing in a whirling dervish of a world.

We thought sure our house was going to tumble down. It was swaying and creaking, glass was breaking inside and we could hear water splashing and the sound of things falling but when it was all over and we staggered weakly into the house very little had been damaged. We had 2-5 gal. gas cans on the kitchen range filled with water for Dog Food, before the quake. They were only half full after it, and my kitchen floor was flooded. Only one bottle tumbled from a shelf and broke.

A mirror fell from the wall but didn't break and the Coleman lantern still was hanging from its hook. That was all and we were grateful.

There were many aftershocks some of them almost as severe as the first however not as long in duration.

As soon as I realized we were having an earthquake. I looked at my watch and when it was over 8 minutes had elapsed so it was a long one, in fact seemed like hours in place of minutes. We went right to the radio and then is when we trembled in fear. Not a sound on the whole dial span of the radio. Turned to short wave and it was cracking and popping. I ran upstairs and turned on the Radio-Phone it was time by then to meet schedule with G.K.O but not a sound on that crystal. Turned to 2512 and contacted Flat Horn Lake. The ice had broken up in the lake and geysers of mud and sand shot into the air. Everyone there was O.K. but quite shook up and worried about everyone in Anchorage. The suspense of not hearing a sound from there was terrible as you by now know from experience but soon we began to hear reports of down town. Then further & further out, till we were pretty sure everyone in our (family) had a pretty good chance of being O.K. if they were all at home and not down town. We were up till 3:30 A.M. Sat morn listening to reports.

After we determined everything was all right here and had talked to Flat Horn, Joe left with the cat to go to Nick's to see how he was, Joe had just taken Nick home a couple hours before. In fact Joe had just returned and had the cat sitting here beside the house when the earthquake hit, and we watched in horrified fascination while that big heavy cat rolled back and forth 6 and 8 feet each way and we feared it would go over the edge of the hill and down.

The ice broke up in the swamp and there are big fissures and holes covering the entirety of this seven by four mill swamp in front of our house.

No doubt we will have more lakes come summer. They said there is a big crack all around the foot of our hill and I know this hill was pitching and bucking like a wild bronc. It's a miracle the whole hill didn't fall apart and not even a rafter or foundation log was misplaced or loosened.

Joe got only about half way between our place and Lydics when he met Nick coming back. Nick said tell Grandma Nick got scare – he trow (throw) water in fire, and grab gun. Nick tink (think) house gonna fall down for sure, he run out and close do (the) door he said to tell you he sure misses you and wishes you were here. He says also to tell you hello Mother and God Bless you. We haven't been able to get to your house since the quake but it must be O.K. at least Lydic's is and Shan didn't say anything about it not being intact when he flew over.

Shan and Edna flew over and landed on our strip yesterday morning, Shan had flown over Sat. Morn. to check on us and then gone on up the River to check everyone up the line. Said Dick Schmidt was at 20 mile, just flew in on Tue. The Army had to send him back with a chopper because they took him out.

Shan says he is much more friendly and outgoing and he thinks the Service was good for him. Shan also told us the river especially the Susitna is all broken up and ice chunks six feet through are standing in all sorts of shapes and positions and one place a whole sand bar shot up above the Ice and is on top of it. Many places where sand & gravel and glacier mud have shot up through the broken ice and fell back down on top of ice & snow. Right after the quake we heard what we thought was shooting from the sights on the hills above Anchorage then over towards Lyonic then up the river and back towards town and it finally occurred to us it was not shooting at all but ice breaking up all over.

Shan checked on Howard Ross, Cliff Rorsberg the folks at Squentna and on up clear to Ken & Hazel Sorensons trapping cabin. They found every one O.K. but shook up. Kenny & Hazel fear for their lives if the weather stays above freezing and it starts to rain as they are only 4 or 5 feet above the river and big ice jams all below them. Shan also went to Talkeetna and Big Lake. Big Lake is a mass of ice chunks and fissures. The railroad is torn and twisted clear to Talkeetna and the highway is full of slides and fissures & all the bridges are out. Shan didn't see any moose and it is feared many of them were lost in fissures and holes in the rivers and lakes.

We heard a short wave broadcast from the man on Mt. Susitna he said he sure thought he was gonna fall off that perch. That old Mt. was really pitching and rolling and it was all they could do to grab ahold and hang on. I don't envy him any. It was bad enough down here without being up there. Joe wants me to tell you it felt to him like being in a big walnut shell out in the ocean.

The ham operators and everyone have done marvelous work and we are proud of the way everyone is arising to the occasion so efficiently. Saturday there were no small planes flying out of Anchorage on account of bad weather but yesterday Roy brought Bill out to check on us and it was a big relief to see them, I'll tell you. Saturday was Randy's 7th birthday and I guess we will all remember it for a good long time. We had hoped they would be out this week end being it was Easter and Randy's birthday too, but of course, the Earthquake fixed that. Guess the kids had a good time anyway as Pat, Dick and family stayed at their house as they had the only cooking facilities in the neighborhood. Propane and water was only off shortly and also electricity was on often enough Bill could turn on furnace and get house good & warm before lights out again.

They used water out of hot water tank for drinking and the only damage to house they sustained was the hot water tank broke loose and went through the wall into living room. Bill had to turn water off and convert the tank again and when he turned water back on there was none but they used what was in tank and melted snow and boiled it so got through nicely.

Bill said the house looked like it was made of rubber and was stretching in every direction during the quake. He said he had Randy and Audie had Laciene and they were outside holding on to each other and the whole world was pitching & rolling and all the houses, too.

He said the car was rolling back & forth & bouncing up & down.

It must have been terrifying. Dick had to go down & check grocery supplies at several places. He's working for a wholesaler now and Bill went with him. He said the devastation is terrible and much more so than they are saying anything about here and there is bound to be much more death toll than mentioned at present. Bill also was just dumbfounded after flying over Turnagain & Mt. McKenzey, up above there a lot of the bluffs are in the Inlet and Shan said all the bluffs up the river are sheared off except the Point at the sand bar. Most of Government Hill is in Knick Arm. All the schools damaged but I suppose you have more news on this than we do, and we haven't seen any of the pictures, of course.

I baked a cake & made ice cream Saturday, hoping the kids would come but anyway, we had cake and ice cream for all our company yesterday. Nick is staying with us till he gets to feeling better again. He just got back from Anchorage and a check-up at hospital. He just got home in time to miss the quake which sure was a good thing or he would probably been on 4th Ave. too, and gone now.

Will write more some other time.

Grace, Joe & Nick

NOTE: We are grateful to Randy Lydic, who lived the life and provided valuable information.

Gardening

From Chapter 16 in *Building a Better Nest*
By Evelyn Hess

"Oh thrice and four times happy those who plant cabbages." --Rabelais

I lie on the grass by the apple trees watching clouds float by. My back, hands and shoulders ache, but it is a good hurt, earned at my favorite pastime: puttering in the garden. Earlier in the day, I squished aphids, thinking of Mother. "That's how you get a green thumb," she said. I feel a bit guilty keeping the bugs from the birds, but our birds seem to prefer the strawberries. I weeded, applied fresh mulch, thinned new plantings, pruned the grapes, and planted seeds until I could work no longer. Then, inhaling the good air, I flopped down rather than trekking back up to the house to rest.

From here I can still admire the foliage, fruits and flowers, smell the warm earth, the tomato leaves, the oregano, feel the sweet breeze playing with my hair, caressing my face. Later, if I am hungry, raspberries, strawberries, peas, beans or kale will be much more seductive than would a peanut butter sandwich in the house. Or I can eat the weeds! So many are edible: the sorrel, nipplewort, clover, dock, bittercress, miner's lettuce, chickweed, and many others. When at last I trudge up the hill with a basket of cucumbers, squash, beans, corn—things I've planted and tended and now harvest their gifts—I feel like a queen.

Most of my earliest memories involve someone working in the garden. Each spring when the soil had drained enough that it would no longer squish and drip when squeezed, my family began to think about a vegetable garden; then a plow turned the ground into a big brown ocean, with waves of clay calling me to go leaping from the crest of one to the next. It must have been very clayey, because I remember no crumbling soil as I jumped from wave to wave. Neither do I remember being scolded—though I may have had the good sense to avoid being caught.

I remember sitting under the red-currant bush and stuffing hands full of their tiny jeweled goodness into my mouth. And "helping" pick and shell peas, popping pods on the curved spot that just fits your thumb, trying to remember not to put the peas into the compost bucket or the shells in the kettle. Now and then I would ever so carefully slice a pod along its back, so that I could fit tiny sticks cross-wise inside and sail my little pea-pod boats. I tell my grandchildren that we didn't have iPods, we just had pea pods, but they were fun.

I wasn't really supposed to play in the garden, and I obeyed that dictum in the ornamental areas. My parents were rose-growers. The garden of my childhood had rectangular rose beds arranged in rows, with a four-pointed star-shaped bed, featuring a tree rose in the middle. Surrounding the beds, climbing roses crawled on trellises. Daddy tended the roses, pruning, spraying, fertilizing, disbudding. Mother grew species roses from seed and hybridized species and miniatures, then made arrangements with their flowers. Between them, my parents grew several hundred roses to perfection, entering them in shows from Seattle to Eugene, and bringing home piles of ribbons and trophies.

When I was nine, Daddy helped me make a little rose garden of my own, and taught me to bud-graft, an amazing process that made me feel like some kind of wizard. You start by collecting scion wood—stems from the rose you want to increase—in February or March while the leaf buds are still dormant, and store them somewhere cool and dark. In June, when the sap runs actively enough that the bark will slip from the rose stem, you slice a "T"-shaped cut just through the bark, on the outside of a stem, below the bottom leaf bud of the bush that will be the stock plant. Then with a sharp knife (Daddy had a special budding knife) you cut a dormant leaf bud (the small bump on the stem inside the petiole of an expanded leaf) from your scion wood, including a shield-shaped bit of bark around the bud. Next you carefully slip the shield under the flaps of the T-cut, leaving the bud itself exposed. Then you tie the bark firmly above and below the bud with a grafting rubber, and you wait. If you did it right – and you did, because your father was watching closely – the old and the new grow together, and a branch grows from that new bud, bearing flowers of sunset colors, maybe, on a bush whose flowers used to be white.

Also when I was about nine, Mother showed me the globular seed capsules of hardy Cyclamen, each capsule a half-inch brown sphere on a spring-coiled stem. (I didn't know it then, but the genus name is presumably taken from the Greek word for circle, alluding to the spirally twisted stem that pulls the mature seed capsule to the earth). With Mother's encouragement, I harvested the sticky squarish seeds from where they had developed inside the capsule, planted them in baby-food cans with drain holes punched in their bottoms, and sold the seedlings with their pretty marbled foliage to the local supermarket. It might have awakened in me a bit of the entrepreneurial spirit—it certainly was a revelation that someone would pay money for something I had grown. I don't remember any particular delight in earning money, but I do remember the awe I felt looking at the capsules on their little brown springs, and the thrill when the seed I poked in the soil actually made a tiny plant.

And that's what excites me still. The miracle of germination, the thrill of growth and bloom and fruit. And experimentation. Trying something new. Figuring out a better way. Or trying, anyway, even if it doesn't turn out to be better.

We garden on soil that would not be considered God's Gift to Gardeners. Rather than being rich valley soil, where fertility is increased as the river deposits its annual stores, this is land that spent most of its life under the ocean. Once the sea receded to expose Oregon, about twenty-four million years ago, this strip that would become the Coast Range remained a plateau until the end of the Miocene and throughout the Pliocene, seven to 1.8 million years ago, when the Coast Range mountains (along with the Grand Canyon, Hell's Canyon, and the shoulders above the Columbia River Gorge) uplifted. So here in the edges of the Coast Range foothills, we garden on old seamounts—mountains once submerged beneath the ocean--that have benefited only from the nutrients dropped from trees, from the decay of vegetation and other organisms, and from the deposits of erosion. Surprising to me, the soil is not rocky. The underlying mudstone flakes into tiny pieces when it is in the air, above ground, becoming stone no more – just part of the clay. Those old seamounts are somewhere deep in the ground, but we've seen no sign other than the minerals in the clay soil. In order to increase the fertility, we add layer after layer of organic matter, which the soil seems to devour almost as fast as we apply it. But we keep dumping it on.

Creatures assist in adding organic matter to the soil, as well as appreciating what we plant there more than I appreciate their help. Voles devour the roots of our strawberry plants, and my attempts to fight back just seem to encourage them. I read that castor oil does a good job of repelling voles, and find it in a pelletized form. How handy! So, excited that I've finally discovered something that holds promise, I begin shaking pellets down the numerous holes. And hooray! It seems to be working. We find no new holes, and the plants look thriftier. We eagerly await the first fruits of the season, but when they come we think, huh! That's odd. Where is that well-known flavor? Just too early in the season perhaps. Or perhaps not.

"You are what you eat," said Adelle Davis in the 60s—along with many others before and since. And that goes for plants as well as people. These plants have been "eating" castor oil. Have you ever tasted castor oil-flavored strawberries? My advice? Don't!

These strawberries are considered everbearing, which really means that they bear in late spring to early summer, then take time off, and bear again late summer and early fall. For the entire early season the berries taste wretched, good enough for birds and slugs apparently, but that's about all. By fall they are decent. The following year they are okay, but two years later they still don't taste as good as they used to. By now it may be another problem—some nutrient I once gave them that I've since forgotten, perhaps—but it also may be some long-lingering residue of castor oil. Some experiments turn out better than others do.

Meanwhile I keep working on the soil in the garden. The current fall-winter regimen on all non-bearing beds is to layer on spoiled straw that an unfortunate neighbor baled right before an early summer rainstorm, then sprinkle on some fertilized sawdust, cover with damp newspapers, and bury it all in leaves.

I put in the new season's garden in June, late as usual, and appreciate that winter cover. The adjoining bed is bare. I'll call it a controlled experiment rather than confessing I didn't finish the fall-mulching program. The covered bed is weed-free, and the soil yields easily to my hoe as I prepare rows. The "control" bed requires a mattock, and each blow jars my body and makes my ears ring. It reminds me of trying to garden a sidewalk. But seed by seed the little plants break through, and in a month or two, the "sidewalk" end of the garden looks no less thrifty than that in the end with the winter mulch.

The garden is my entertainment, my hobby, my exercise, my joy. It also helps keep us healthy and is a small contribution to the health of the earth. Organic matter added to the soil enlists the aid of arthropods and microorganisms to break it down, supplying a steady stream of nutrients to the soil and building the first step for a balanced system. Conventional agriculture often sterilizes the soil, tills it – breaking up the soil ecosystem – adds petroleum-based fertilizers, and doesn't renew the soil with compost. As the soil becomes depleted, damaging insects and diseases proliferate. So chemicals are sprayed on to kill the bugs and disease, killing the beneficials while they're at it. Like people who are dependent on pharmaceuticals – with pills for the side effects of other pills – instead of the healing power of their own bodies, these soils become dependent on the chemical cycle. Then the produce is shipped a couple thousand miles, losing freshness as it goes and adding that much more CO_2 to the atmosphere.

Organic homegrown produce, or produce purchased from a local farmers' market, can be eaten fresh from the garden, losing few of its nutrients. It is free of chemical sprays, and full of vitamins and minerals. We benefit; the insects benefit; the soil benefits.

And so I continue this work that gives me pleasure, that helps sustain us, and that reminds me of my parents. Season by season, year by year, successes and failures, delight and sadness, I happily ride this amazing carousel of life.

An Evening With Michele O. - Under Glass
By Marv Himmel

He took one last deep breath trying valiantly to make himself taller, more manly. This was the moment he dreaded. His hands trembled slightly as he stepped toward her, a long sharp straight pin dancing furiously in his right hand, an orchid corsage quivering in the other. He was going to pin the orchid on her dress... on her chest... on her breast. Oh! My God! He had never done anything like this before. Until now the only way he had ever touched a girl he liked was by punching her on the shoulder or pulling her hair. He nearly collapsed in relief when her mother stepped forward to take the pin and flower from his hands. He wasn't sure if she was being kind or just afraid of seeing her eldest daughter bleed to death in front of her.

Tonight was Westfir High's Sweetheart's Ball. It was his first real date and he was taking Michele O., his "older woman," to the dance. He was a mere high school freshman while she was a sophomore. Not only that, she was from Chicago and she was smart and she was nice and standing there with her long dark hair hanging over her shoulders and wearing a crimson print dress, black-rimmed cat's-eye glasses and looking at him with her wonderful little smile, the one where the corners of her mouth turned up ever so slightly; she was beautiful!

Years later, the images and sensations from that Oregon evening in 1958 played out in his mind like some silent, amateur art film. He was of an age now when he had far more memories than plans. Perhaps the snowflakes drifting down outside the window were the trigger.

In his mind he could see the white and green 1954 Chevrolet Biscayne drive from out of the darkness and park in front of her house under the single street light hanging overhead. A young man, a boy really, dressed in his older brother's slightly too large sport coat got out of the car, turned to say something to the driver and, carrying a small white cardboard box, hurried toward the front porch to get out of the cold, rainy February evening. He hesitated for a moment then reached out and pushed the doorbell.

High school dances were held in the multipurpose cafeteria-auditorium-theater just off to the right as you entered the building. That evening, rolls of red and white crepe paper flounces hung from the high ceiling and construction paper hearts were taped artfully along the walls. Lunch tables were collapsed into their receptacles and metal folding chairs lined the sides of the room. Near the front, pushed against the wall, a single linen covered table held a large crystal bowl of red steaming punch, a mixture of 7-Up, raspberry sherbet and dry ice. On the stage, a large, padded wingback chair sat between the half-open curtains where later in the evening the Queen of the Ball would be officially crowned. On the far end, an entire wall of windows looked out over the green wet grass of the practice field. Two large flood lamps mounted on the outside upper corners lit the field well enough so that from the dimmed room inside you could see a row of trees and the river beyond and, up by the lights, the fine mist of rain settling steadily down.

That awkward first dance. This wasn't like the dancing they made you do in PE class where they randomly paired off boys and girls and tried to teach you how to waltz while a scratchy recording of "The Blue Danube" blared across the gymnasium floor and echoed off the basketball backboards. No, this was much more serious. This was a real dress-up, go-with-a-girl-you-really-like, dance!

The music began to play. Slow music. They looked at one another, he nodded ever so slightly and together they started toward the center of the dance floor. She turned toward him and put her hand on his left shoulder. He reached around her waist to the small of her back and grasped her other hand in his. His fingertips, suddenly acute sensors, could feel the tight weave of her dress, the line of the zipper down her back, the subtle undulation of her hips when she moved and the warm moistness of her hand in his. He could feel her multi-layered petticoats performing their matronly duties as they pushed back against his knees. He was surprised at how strong, how solid and supple her back felt under his hand.

Tentatively he stepped forward trying to find the rhythm and they began. They didn't look at each other at first, instead they looked out over their outstretched arms as though preparing to tango and began to move with a stiff, stilted, jerkiness more like stick figures, around and around, until gradually relaxing and beginning to move together, one leading, the other following, they danced. House rules, strictly enforced, maintained that there would be no cheek-to-cheek bodily contact but as the evening deepened, as the dancing improved and the shyness retreated, they began to look at one another and as they did they moved in as closely as they could.

"That's okay, I walk on them too!" was the only criticism his dancing received the entire evening.

Midway through the dance, snow began to fall. At first, through the floodlights, you could see small occasional flakes mixed in with the winter rain but as the evening progressed more and more of the mix turned to snow until outside the windows the night-lit sky was filled with silver dollar flakes and the grass slowly covered in a quiet white blanket so that by the end, a full three-inch layer softened everything.

He had arranged for them to be let off several blocks away so they could walk for a time through the falling snow. At this late hour, the newly-covered side streets were unblemished by tire tracks, foot traffic, or even pets. They were as pure and fresh as the two youngsters who, holding hands, came walking out from the darkness into the circle of light under the street lamp in front of her home while the snowflakes continued touching down lightly on her dark hair and blending with the tiny white roses of her red print dress.

They stopped in the shadows just to the side of porch. He hesitated for a moment then leaned forward and kissed her quickly, gently on her lips and then shyly turned and hurried away through the falling snow out of the light and into the night to walk the remainder of the way to his own home. He did not notice the cold. He did not notice the falling snow.

He did have a smile on his face.

And many years later, the old man in the chair by the window looking out at the falling snow, smiled too.

Photo Gallery

"Brothers." Author John Henry (left) and his brother Jim, ca 1948, in Michigan. *Photo courtesy of John Henry*

A Kitchen History
By Reida Kimmel

I recently acquired a worn notebook written in my grandmother's hand, containing menu plans for the first half of 1911. I never knew my grandparents, but I knew enough about their lives to entertain certain expectations about the contents of that book. Perhaps I'd find an American version of Downton Abbey's cuisine. My grandfather, 'Pa,' born shortly before the Civil War, grew up on a farm. His two older brothers started a small mill manufacturing quilts. Many of those quilts traveled west with homesteaders' families. Pa joined the business, but making 'comforters' was not satisfying enough. He traveled around in a wagon with a young cabinetmaker named Israel Sack. They bought old junk furniture from the farmers in Connecticut and Rhode Island, cleaned it up and sold it. Today we call that 'junk' priceless Americana – Chippendale, Queen Anne and Pilgrim Century furniture. Early in the twentieth century, the affluent were just beginning to appreciate the beauty and rarity of American antiques. The family business that Israel Sack started in 1905 came to be the nation's most respected and pricey antique store. My grandfather became wealthy, but he remained in New London, Connecticut, in 'Westomere,' a large Arts and Crafts style house on spacious grounds. Here he displayed and sold his antiques. His wife Neva Ffenno – 'Ma' – was the daughter of an innkeeper in the Finger Lakes region of New York State. She was a dark and handsome woman of suitably operatic proportions, who gave up her singing career to become the second wife of a much older man. They had three daughters, Neva, my mother, Janna, and baby Priscilla. Mother remembered that there were servants, including a gardener. She adored her father, an affable man, fond of pie for breakfast. Every year, Grandfather Ffenno visited, and he and Pa went off in the wagon buying chickens to ship to New York State for the restaurant. "The best chickens come from Connecticut," they said. After the girls were grown, Pa and Ma sold Westomere and moved to a smaller place near the shore. The house was torn down during the Depression, and replaced with a block of modest houses close to my childhood home.

Did this nouveau riche couple entertain and feast lavishly? No, for the most part, they clung to their culinary roots, enjoying good plain country cooking. New Years Day, page one, and they are having baked beans, brown bread, and bacon for breakfast. Those baked beans are still a family favorite, though we have them for dinner. Brown bread was Grandfather Ffenno's specialty, soda bread, laden with salt and sugar, but made with whole-wheat flour, which was unusual in those days. The family ate meat, chicken or fish at every meal, and as spring arrived, shellfish, including lobster. Potatoes and surprisingly, sweet potatoes, figured prominently. Many dishes were creamed. Broth was popular to start a dinner. Janna and Baby drank a lot of broth, while Neva got few vegetables and lots of chops and potatoes. Ma planned three meals a day, no lavish teas or appetizers. 'Dinner' was the midday meal with 'supper' in the evening. Leftovers were used and used again. Boiled dinner became cold corned beef and then corned beef hash. Steak reappeared as hash or pie. My mother taught me two rules for cooking. "1) nothing wasted; 2) everything made from scratch." Now I know where she learned those lessons.

The family could afford anything that was available, but in winter, the choices were limited to winter vegetables – beets, parsnips, carrots, celery and turnips. The beans, peas, asparagus, corn and lima beans on the menus were probably canned, as were the tomatoes. My 1906 edition of Fanny Farmer's Boston Cooking School Cookbook, probably my grandmother's, as she wrote her name on the ripped title page, has clever hints for cooking with canned vegetables. Fanny tells us that though fresh beans and spinach are available all year, they are not good. The Palmers ate fruit and vegetables at every meal, salads of celery and apples, applesauce, baked apples, stewed tomatoes. How joyful they must have been when dandelions, the first spring greens, became available in early March. Cultivated dandelion greens appeared on the menu often. Wild dandelions would not appear until late spring in New England. Did my grandparents have a greenhouse? Soon they were eating beet greens, and on April 18th "asparagus [fresh]" as well as watercress salad appeared on the dinner menu.

A century ago this upper middle class family ate an overly caloric but remarkably healthy diet in spite of the fact that food availability was limited to local food and produce shipped from market gardens a few hundred miles to the south. [Fanny Farmer mentions that produce of very dubious quality is shipped fresh from California and Florida.] Beside the pleasure of glimpsing into the daily workings of a household in 1911, can we take home any lessons from these frail pages? How dissimilar are our meal planning options? Today I can go to the store and buy all sorts of fresh produce like asparagus, corn, sweet peppers, grapes, or peaches and plums, at any time of the year. But in winter these items come from Chile, Peru, Central America and Mexico. Like Fanny Farmer I can disparage their quality, but there is a greater issue at stake. Those items cost fuel to get here. Buy Peruvian asparagus or Chilean grapes and you are buying into global warming. Use restraint and wait for fresh local asparagus and fruits, and they will taste all the better for being longed for. We might not think of ourselves as wealthy, but we are so rich in choices, in food, in travel opportunities, in entertainment, so able to indulge ourselves, that we are really very similar to those old Palmers with their staff of servants, their lovely gardens and spoiled children. I admire the way Ma and Pa clung to their culinary roots even when they were wealthy. We can learn a bunch of lessons from them about creatively using what the season has to offer. Ma's cook had to buy local and seasonal. For us, we have to retrain ourselves to do so. That is easy here in Oregon where just about every-thing good can grow, except for citrus, coffee and bananas. Those, inciden-tally, were the sole exotic items on the Palmer winter menus.

My mother chose to go to cooking school, Fanny Farmer's of course, instead of college. Needless to say, she was a wonderful cook, meticulous but creative. The following are old family recipes that she passed on to me, the old way, by word and example.

Connecticut Baked Beans

Saturday night supper, or a great holiday side dish with ham, chicken or turkey.

You need a good heavy 4 quart cooking pot with a lid. Two pounds of beans, small red, kidney, or navy. Cover with 2 quarts of water and let soak overnight.

The next day, drain the beans and then replace them in the pot, covering them generously with water. Cook the beans until the skins wrinkle and burst when you blow on them. Drain, reserving the cook-ing liquid.

Cover ½ pound of salt pork with boiling water. Soak 2 minutes and then drain the pork. Slash one-inch long gashes in the fat but do not cut through the rind. Alternately replace the salt pork with ½ pound of good lean bacon cut in 2 inch slices and similarly soaked in hot water and then drained.

Push the pork or bacon down in the bean pot.

Mix 1 teaspoon of salt, ½ cup of brown sugar, I teaspoon dry mustard, ¼ teaspoon ground cloves, ¼ teaspoon cinnamon, and two or three inches of fresh orange peel. Stir into a pint of the reserved cooking water. Pour over the beans. Add water to cover the beans, us-ing up the reserved cooking water first.

Cover the pot and bake six to eight hours at 250 degrees. Do not let the beans dry out. Add water as needed. If the beans seem too moist, remove the lid for the last hour or two of the cooking.

Real Chowders

Traditionally chowders were made with potatoes not flour as the thickener, gluten free and perfectly delicious! For approximately 5 cups of chowder.

Two ounces of lean bacon cut up into 1-inch pieces

One large or two medium potatoes, peeled and diced. Russet or yellow Finn are both good. [about 10 ounces of prepared potatoes]

One medium onion diced. [Three or four ounces]

Half a carrot diced

A four inch piece of celery diced. [optional]

Two 6.5 ounce cans of minced or chopped clams

OR... 12 ounces of fresh clams chopped

OR... 12 ounces of firm fleshed fish like cod, salmon, rockfish or halibut

OR... a mix of canned clams, fresh fish, and even shrimp. This is 'slumgullion'

Milk, preferably not skim, or half and half, to taste

Have your ingredients prepared, simmer the bacon gently till it gives off its juices and add the onions. Swirl them around to heat and soften for several minutes, and add the potatoes, carrot and optional celery. Toss them with the onion and bacon, and cover all with water, just enough to cover the mix. Put the lid on the pot and simmer10 or 15 minutes till the potatoes are soft enough to mash but not mushy. Remove and put aside 1/3 of the bacon vegetable mix. Mash the rest very thoroughly. Return the other vegetables and add the can or cans of clams. Heat but do not boil. Add the raw seafood if you are using it and a little water, heat to near boiling. Stirring gently add the milk, usually one third to one half a cup, [more if you are not using clams and their juices] until the chowder becomes a nice rich thickness. Add salt and black pepper to taste.

Looking for Milk, I Found a Rose
By Elaine Kost

Friendship like a flower
can bloom into something beautiful
with the right amount of sunshine and rain.

Who would have thought that an ad on Craigslist could bring two people together and bond them like family? Who do I thank? Does Craigslist have a rating system like Amazon – one where I comment and rate my experience? They should. Maybe I ought to suggest a blog of shared stories like mine.

It started one day when I learned about posting an ad. My husband and I enjoy goat's milk and if at all possible we wanted to buy directly from the farm. We had been buying raw goat's milk from the local market, but thought we could do better than the price of $9.99 a half gallon and we know from the food we grow ourselves, nothing beats fresh. The milk we were buying still had a bit of a "goaty taste."

About a week after I put the ad on Craigslist, the phone rang. Rose introduced herself and said she was responding to our ad and the price would be $8 a gallon. I was questioned right away whether I would be an ongoing customer and didn't know how to answer as I hadn't seen the operation. Was it clean? Were the goats cared for in a humane way? Were the methods they used for healing more holistic than not?

I understood why Rose asked. She explained how they package the milk for their regular customers in previously frozen bags so it would remain cold during their journey home. If we were just wanting to try it, then she would forego putting the milk in these bags and asked that I bring a cooler.

Arrangements were made and directions to the house were explicit, even the part about the turn into the driveway being a little sharp coming from my direction. I drove down a long, gravel driveway, taking in the surroundings as I approached a home surrounded by trees – big beautiful trees – and I couldn't help but wonder what I would find beyond the door.

Today, some four years later, I can say with certainty that I never expected to find so much love and compassion under a single roof. I met a mother and daughter team taking care of their loved ones and managing a small goat herd, all of whom I got to meet; Lily, Lady and Zlinda, their Saanen delights.

I was greeted at the door with more than a smile and there was an energy that filled me with excitement, something no price would ever pay for.

Rose offered me a taste of the milk and I was so surprised that it tasted like milk and not goats. "It's so creamy and delicious, I said, It doesn't have that goaty taste at all."

Rose smiled and said, "It shouldn't if it's fresh."

My milk was packaged in a red freezer bag, one gallon. We then discussed what day would be good for me to stop on a regular basis. Little did I know that our acquaintance would turn into a lasting friendship.

Each week that went by, I looked forward to my pickup and before long I was making my own Ricotta and Mozzarella cheese. I was unfamiliar with whey and all of its wonderful uses. My bread enjoyed its addition and our smoothies came alive.

Rose and I discovered we had more in common than enjoying the outdoors, making things with our own hands and caring for others (including four-legged ones). Our enthusiasm grew as we shared learning new things together. We learned we were alike in ways that are unusual in our "techy" world. We are content at being home in our little "nests" that, over the years, have taken on our character; all who enter are welcome.

I believe, though, the bond that ties our friendship with the biggest and brightest bow is helping others. Whether it's caring for a loved one who is ill, teaching someone who has the interest to learn, or sharing information that may help someone else's first-time experience be a pleasant one.

As part of my once-a-week trip to town, I would visit a hospice patient. Sometimes it was spent laughing over a comedy together, reading to someone who wasn't necessarily listening or just holding the hand of someone I never knew before. Rose was caring for two elderly gentlemen who were/are (one has since passed) very important to her and we both found that giving was something that came naturally for us. Her daughter is an amazing example of a young woman that has learned many of the skills needed to keep a homestead on acreage maintained, and together, they have worked hand in glove.

Since that first trip down a gravel driveway to collect milk, not only have we indulged in homemade eats together, we have laughed and cried while sharing deep feelings of love, sadness and joy. I seldom left without fresh cookies to eat on the way home, or homemade caramel to top my ice cream. And before Rose taught me how to make my own, there was always a surprise of fresh ricotta in the side pocket of the bag.

Our visits grew longer and I began to see how the routines of her life preempted time for herself. Watching her caring for two loved ones full time, both needing help with the basic things in life made me think about ways I could help.

I cherish my time that allows me to enjoy my crafts of knitting, hardanger embroidery and spinning. I wondered if there was something I could teach Rose that she didn't already know how to do, something that wouldn't require a block of time, per se, but time that flowed, something fluid.

Then one day while sitting at my wheel spinning a soft fleece that would become a sweater, the light went on. I know the joy of spinning. A fluid motion of hands and feet, a meditation practice that provides one with warmth. My next visit I would offer to teach Rose how to spin.

There was little that I had to say to convince Rose about spinning. My Ashford Traditional wheel went with me on my next visit and I explained to her I was in no hurry to get it back. I assured her that it would be awkward at first and like most things there is no substitute for practice. After a couple of mini lessons, I could tell Rose was determined enough to stay with it and before long I saw progress on the bobbin.

Rose was a natural, a professional seamstress by trade, her hands knew what to do almost immediately and her smile lit up her eyes at the yarn that became her own.

Since we met, we've enjoyed sharing so many things together. Everything from fixing a microwave door to making drapes for our new residence here in Southern Oregon (doing the latter over the phone and in emails with pictures). We continue to share our lives and I look forward to another trip north to sit face to face, enjoying milk and cookies.

I'm so fortunate to have someone who feels as I do about life, love and relationship. I love my brothers, but I always wanted a sister. I never knew what that would feel like until I met Rose. Our communication with each other is unlike any other women friends I've had. She has made me a better listener; not just because I can learn so much from her, but because I know when I need someone to hear me, and she does.

Since we've moved, I miss our weekly visits and our face time. I miss seeing everyone else (two- and four-legged) who live on the property; her loved ones who know that they couldn't be loved more. The goats are cared for in a loving manner, fed sprouted grains and healed with herbs when needed. They are taken on walks in the woods and are give the utmost attention when their babies are born.

I miss the trip down the gravel driveway, and last but certainly not least, I miss the fresh, raw milk from their loved Saanen goats. Thank you, Craigslist, for enriching my life with product and love.

Selfie at Seventy-Seven
By Demetri Liontos

At lunch the other day a friend suggested we preserve the memory of the delicious Thai food we'd just devoured. He whipped out his smartphone and took several selfies from different angles. The food. The table. The two grinning faces. "I'll email them to you," he said. I thought no more about it until later that evening when I checked my updates and indeed, there they were—four shots in dazzling colors of two carefree guys and the ruins of our Pad Thai lunch. I had no trouble recognizing my friend, but who was the other guy? Not me, surely.

A funny thing happens to you on your way through your seventies: You lose track of what you look like. Changes occur at an impossible speed. Hair goes from a chic salt and pepper to gunmetal gray to Santa Claus white. And alarmingly less of it. Bags under eyes appear permanently packed for a long trip to who knows where. Even a smile, once jaunty and generous, now looks strained, impatient for the photo shoot to end. When did this happen? How did this happen? And to me, of all people. (Well, most of us, I think, believe in our immortal specialness, don't we?)

As if these physical aberrations weren't enough, the less noticeable mental ones rear up unbidden and often. This lets you know you're closer to the end than the beginning. (Not that your math, ever cold and uncaring, didn't already confirm that.) Those frequent trips standing in front of the fridge wondering what you wanted. Forgetting your neighbor's name in the middle of the funny (to you) story you were telling. Sending a second thank-you card, unsure if you sent the first one. Losing focus in a friendly conversation. Soon, you can't dodge it. Things are indeed changing—fast and not necessarily for the better. Still, there's a part of you that shouts, "What, get older? Naw, not me. Never!"

I hadn't planned on living forever, and judging by my parents' early demise, my genes are betting against it. At my seventy-seventh birthday recently, I had the bittersweet feeling of having outlived my father by fifteen years and being a year away from my mother's age when she died. Friends drank to my health and told me I looked great—for my age. Are there national or even international standards for how people should look at a given age? If so, we could stick them on our fridge as a guide to live up to. And this, possibly, as we reach for one of those naughty snacks that can only derail us. Looking in the mirror reminds us of that.

At seventy-seven, rolling off the tongue as it does, most of the people I know are younger and inflicted with the disorder communicators love to hate: the generation gap. Technologies soar. Fashions push the envelope. Social mores crumble. But the ancient notion of a generation gap stands tall and palpable. Half a lifetime as a teacher in college and public education has only confirmed that. (After all, the teacher is almost always older than the student; it's the principle of mentoring.) Is it possible to have close friends, say, ten or twenty years younger? Of course. The gap cuts both ways, and the only impediment is how much of your respective universes will you have to explain to carry on a decent conversation. This takes patience and openmindedness. Not for the faint of heart but usually worth it.

How about those older folks? Well, what's scary about them is: That's where you're going! Ugh, those liver spots. Didn't your mother teach you not to drool? And the endless litany of physical ailments! Gawd, how come you're still alive? Well, my mother-in-law also had a birthday recently, her ninety-fifth. She lives alone and "does for herself." She shuffles on her walker now where not long ago she danced up a storm. And when my wife and I forget a birthday, she's there to remind us. With no notes or smartphone to prompt her. Growing old gracefully can be more than a cliche.

You also know you're getting older by changes of interest. Things you did once you don't or can't do now. I once climbed half a dozen Northwest mountains in the space of a few years. A backpacking buddy asked me last summer to go to Mount Jefferson Park, scene of some memorably spectacular outings in our sixties. Love to, except that I can't carry a pack any more. Sad, yes. Natural, also yes. My wife complains of not going out dancing as we used to. I smile sheepishly and give her my standard line. Of course we'll go dancing again. We're not dead yet!

And perhaps that's the carrot that keeps us going. We know it's going to happen. It hasn't yet. It could at any time. So I'll live the cliché: Live every day as though it were your last. And do it gracefully, right Mom?

Joey

By Norm Maxwell

Sometime in 2006, my wife Sande came home with her arm bleeding. I asked her what the story was and she said she tried to grab an abandoned cat at the beginning of Fire Road where we lived near Lorane. In that moment, I realized that we had just adopted another cat, so I grabbed a can of food and a pet carrier. We drove the couple of miles to where the road connects with Siuslaw River Road and Sande got out and called "Kitty, Kitty, Kitty!"

Sure enough, I saw a half-grown black cat skulking around the edge of the beet field next to the road. He was clearly very hungry and it didn't take too long to lure him into the cat carrier with an open can of Friskies. We had seen black cats down the road at "Dogpatch," so we figured he must be from there.

We called him Kitten for a time, as in "Ben," (one of our other cats) "don't beat on the kitten!" The little black cat liked to hide in his cat carrier where he felt safe, so I dubbed him Joey after Uncle Joey from the "Back to the Future" movies. He liked to play roughly with Aunt Gus, the Maine Coon cat, but Ben the Bengal was in his prime and was not to be trifled with by a young Delta cat.

Joey loved to play in a cat-sized tent that Sande bought. It had a coarse weave in the fabric that he could see through. While other cats would sometimes sleep in it, Joey preferred to lurk inside it and then leap at unsuspecting cats or people. The tent would tumble across the floor at you and the other cats found this disconcerting.

The years passed and a grey tortoiseshell adopted us. She came with the name Amelia and I soon modified it to Antisocial Amy as she wanted nothing to do with the other cats. Ben didn't like her one little bit and would try to chase her away. Joey tried to be her friend, but was constantly rebuffed.

AA liked to play sometimes and Joey would hear her thrashing around with a catnip mouse and come running to see if she wanted to play with him. She would hiss loudly and eventually he quit trying to be her friend. Aunt Gus eventually died and then one day last summer, Antisocial Amy disappeared. Since cougars were seen in the neighborhood, we chose to believe that she had been eaten by one. She never missed a meal or strayed further than 50 yards from the house.

Ben got old. He was no longer hell on wheels and Joey would wash the old Bengal's

The entire Klatt family extends our heartfelt thank you to Norman Maxwell (and "Joey" the Cat) of Lorane, Oregon for the heroic act of rescuing of our 91 year old mother from her burning house.

Forever thankful-
Joe, Karen, Katherine, James, and the entire family.

Sunday, June 14, 2015
Register-Guard

ears. He sometimes even brought his friend a vole to catch after Ben went blind. I made the call to terminate Ben at home in time for Memorial Day weekend and Joey found himself an only cat.

Early this past D-Day morning, Joey mewed and pulled at the covers for me to get up and let him outside. This had been a ritual for the past few months when Joey, Ben and I would all go outside to pee anywhere from 0200 to 0400. Then we would all go back in the house and return to bed. I would always take a powerful flashlight and at least a .44 pistol with me and look around for cougars. Frequently I would see deer bedded down in the lawn.

This time, Joey disappeared into the the darkness and so I had to make sure there were no mountain lions hanging around the yard. I walked around the north end of the house and saw fire through the fir privet hedge. I could tell it was coming from the neighboring house's porch. I ran back in my house and called 911 before running over there. Time was needlessly wasted on the phone, but everybody got out of the house unharmed, and the Lorane Volunteer Fire Department arrived to keep the fire from spreading.

I helped relocate the old woman and her caregiver to her daughter's house in Lorane. When I returned home, there was Joey sitting on the porch in the dawn.

I got to thinking about it and was totally amazed at the timing of Joey wanting to go out. The bathroom window was open. Did he hear the fire and smell the smoke and know I needed to get up? Did God tell him to wake me up? Or did his bladder tell him it was time to go out?

Joey isn't saying.

Discovering the Game of Bingo
By Thomas Oroyan

Nearly two years ago, my wife gael showed me an article by Groundwaters' editor, Pat Edwards, telling of the letter she wrote to a radio personality, protesting something he said on the radio. The guy was trying to be funny when he cracked the following riddle/joke: "How do you get 200 cows in a barn? – You put up a bingo sign!" According to Pat, it insinuated that players of bingo where merely obese women who would go anywhere to play bingo, which made Pat livid... and rightly so. The portrayal is so untrue, especially in this day and age. I agree wholeheartedly with Pat. In fact her response inspired me to write my own experiences and views of the game for a writing class that I take at the Campbell Center.

As a kid in grade school, my brother and I would try to sneak in and watch the people play bingo at the community or church parish halls. At that time, they were mostly elderly women players. At the church bingos, we would pretend to look for our parents who didn't participate, but we were really watching the games and what took place. We were taken by the ambiance. The church hall filled with people sitting on long wood benches at long tables. They chatted as they marked their paper cards and filled the air with tobacco smoke. We were in awe of the shelves lined with prizes for the winners including dishes, bowls, blankets, baskets of goodies and more. Eventually we were shooed away by an adult. We came away thinking the game seemed simple enough and wondered why we kids weren't allowed to play.

Three years ago, at the age of 72 and a year into my second marriage, I finally got my chance to play bingo when my wife gael asked me go with her to the local charity bingo hall. gael's daughter found out our bingo nights were starting to become regularly scheduled nights out and exclaimed "Oh my God! She's corrupted him!"

After attending a dozen games, about once or twice a week, I found to my surprise that the game was not only fun but interesting, simple yet challenging. I found it tasked my concentration and helped my hand and eye coordination. Socializing goes on before, during and after the games. We met a lot of people. Being new to Eugene, and of course, gael being gael, she made new friends quickly. We enjoyed finding commonalities with some of the players, i.e other writers, class students, neighbors, fellow island people or people from other bingo halls. The bingo game seems contagious and seems to pop up at places we frequent and enjoy like the senior centers, coast casinos and the cruise ships we travel on.

Hopefully being intelligent people, gael and I are aware and do remind ourselves that Bingo is a gambling game, a game of chance. So we take this fun outing as entertainment and budget likewise. We don't expect to win big money and know that "the house" has the odds to eventually collect more than your winnings. However, when you do win, it's fun and you get an adrenaline rush when you yell "Bingo!" Caveat however...

being a game of chance, probabilities may not go your way. You may go several bingo nights without a win and thus a good chance for boredom to creep in. So skip bingo for awhile, thus allowing for a good break and another activity.

There appears a stigma still, that Bingo is a woman's game. For example, Bob, who usually sits at the next table in back of us during games at the Arc. Bob is heavy-set and burly looking, about 6' 2" tall and a bachelor in his fifties. One night, we noticed him sharing laughter with a couple of players who were teasing him for carrying his bingo bag in a paper sack. When asked why, he said, "Well, with my basket-like bingo bag containing daubers with its bright multi-colored caps conspicuously sticking out, it just didn't look too 'macho.' It would spoil my image."

Interesting to note that I've observed some men carrying their colorful bingo daubers in a small carry-on bag or a knapsack, or they just stick a bunch of daubers in their jacket pockets. Some are lucky enough to be married and the wife carries the dauber basket. Maybe men would not be so intimidated if some women didn't make a project out of their dauber baskets. Some decorate them with bright numbers and flowers, adding and adorned with fake flowers and good luck charms – many, little stuffed dolls and animals.

I'm not one to throw stones at a guys' hesitancy in carrying a colorful basket with colorful daubers. Recently I found it strangely uncomfortable when gael asked me to carry our colorful basket on my lap while she pushed my wheelchair into the bingo establishment. I remember waiting at the table we chose to settle while gael stood in line to get bingo cards. An elderly woman stopped to admire our bingo basket and asked questions on how it was made. I answered, mimicking gael's answer she gives to others, "A friend made it out of plastic bags and wove it into a basket... clever and pretty, isn't it?'"

I thought to myself... "Gee, I'm making small talk with a nice elderly lady on pretty basket weaving?" I did gain a friend who waves and says "hi" every time I see her now.

I see all age groups, from different backgrounds and education, playing bingo now. Bingo players are not a class of people. They come from all walks of life and cannot be stereotyped. Most like to socialize, which is why they go to bingo, and I'm sure most also enjoy other similar competitive group activities that combine fun and friends.

The bottom line? Bingo is fun for everyone.

On a Dark and Stormy Night
By Rachel Rich

On a boot-black night, Mom, Kris and I shelled dried beans, while Dad read us *The Strange Case of Doctor Jekyll and Mr. Hyde*. This dark tale by Robert Lewis Stevenson was from our collection of *Great Books* by Britannica, which happened to share a shelf beside alien and Sasquatch literature. With thunder and lightning pealing outside and Halloween just around the corner, the atmosphere was spooky and the timing apt. Mom spiced up the fun with fragrant cinnamon pumpkin cake and steaming cocoa. After taking an Evelyn Wood Speed Reading Course, Dad had over-come his shyness about reading aloud, making his dramatic rendition of Stevenson singularly memorable. For Halloween week, listening to Jekyll and Hyde became the cherry on the cake of our free time.

On more typical evenings, when we weren't doing our own thing, we'd play Yahtzee or Monopoly, or use the Ouija Board. But more often we'd putter, fix things, knit or do light chores, entertaining each other with stories, book discussions or debates about far-out topics. Without Jekyll and Hyde lurking in the shadows, we'd have merely discussed crop circles, UFO's or Sasquatch. But who knew we'd stumble across the Shaggy Shuffler – in person!

Around 1973, Peter Byrne, an author and self-styled Bigfoot guru, planted his museum trailer at the foot of a butte just west of The Dalles, Oregon. A mysterious event lured him to this obscure spot: against a rosy sunset, locals spotted the silhouette of a burly beast with big feet, as he lumbered across a ridge not far from Mom's folks. While visiting Grampa and Gramma Luthy, I just couldn't pass up the opportunity to view Byrne's museum with its renowned deceased Bigfoot and to meet the author of a book Mom's family often discussed, *The Search for Bigfoot: Monster, Myth or Man*. Word was Byrne shipped Bigfoot straight from the Smithsonian! Strangely, we subscribed to the *Smithsonian Magazine*, yet its January 1974 article "The Search Goes on for Bigfoot" failed to mention either owning this spectacular exhibit or lending it to Byrne.

Never mind. At dusk Dad and I embarked on our pilgrimage, Grampa Dick's '46 pickup wending down old Columbia Highway, dodging boulders fallen from the hillside, then putt-putting up a long, dusty road to halt before an aluminum trailer. More skeptical than I, Dad remained in the Dodge so as not to toss a wet blanket over my enthusiasm and to let me draw my own conclusions. I was a gawking groupie, longing to shake the hand of an internationally published author, then view Mr. Byrne's prized Bigfoot, known to Native Americans as Sasquatch. So I gladly chipped in the entry fee – a paltry $1.50.

How the man kept a straight face, I have no idea. In a long freezer, beneath four inches of hazy ice, slumbered a supposed Sasquatch carcass. Bungling Byrne had crudely stitched together a gorilla costume with patches of cheap, slightly off-hue fake fur with hair pointing up, down and sideways. Clearly he was no taxidermist and I could have done a better job with a pitchfork and baling wire. Out of politeness, I stifled belly laughs until hopping into the truck to share my report. Dad and I giggled like the teenager I was.

That night Grampa Dick fessed up that he personally knew both the Sasquatch and his spotters – infamous jokesters. The Bigfoot silhouette seen cresting the butte was actually a rancher checking his cattle before dark. But mentioning this to the public, let alone to the press, would have spoiled the fun. The hulking rancher tromped around his property in huge cork boots, swinging side-to-side like the logger he'd once been. Adding to the whopper, locals fashioned feet the size of turkey platters to stamp across the hillside. No doubt they laughed like hyenas when Byrne parked his aluminum "museum" nearby to capitalize on their prank.

Now fast forward to a dark and drizzly night decades after my encounter with Byrne. Tonight I googled him only to find an earlier whopper that dragged all kinds of people into his vortex. In 1957, a man named Tom Slick (his real name!), conducted an expedition to search for a Yeti hand in the Buddhist monastery of Pangboche, Nepal. A Yeti is said to be the Asian cousin of Bigfoot. In 1959, Byrne, a Slick associate, stole it from Nepal, where James Stewart (yes, the actor!) smuggled the Yeti hand from India to the US. Then on the 1960 World Book Expedition, Sir Edmund Hillary and Marlin Perkins of TV fame, took a side trip to Nepal to check out the Yeti story, after spying on Chinese rocket launches (really)! Hillary decided Byrne added human bones to what later turned out to be a Neanderthal hand! The truth alone was freaky fantastic, but Byrne felt compelled to throw fact and fiction into a blender and give 'em a whirl. (http://en.wikipedia.org/wiki/Panboche_Hand, April 23, 2014)

Not content to concoct a Nepalese Yeti hand, Byrne chased Yeti's cous- in Bigfoot, all the way to the Northwest, where I met his newest craft project, Freezer Foot. My hilarious adventure with Dad earned me the right to say, "I saw Bigfoot!" (wink, wink, nudge, nudge), before mentioning fake fur. Despite pesky facts, others' pranks fueled years of the Luthy family's debates over the existence of Sasquatch, Yeti or Loch Ness monster. Each new controversy offered all the excitement of discovering a twenty dollar bill in the pocket of an old coat.

Here's a sample of our wacky conversations as we gathered around Dick and Dorothy's dinner table. (Names are changed to protect the guilty.)

Somebody would throw out a line: "I hear Bud went fishing up on Seven Mile Creek and found a big old pile of Sasquatch scat."

"Ooh, gross. We're trying to eat."

Another grabbed the bait, "They say Bigfoot stinks like a bear and bugles like an elk!" adding a high-pitched howl that made everybody jump. "Even Juanita, the neighbor, says Sasquatch is eating her cats."

A guffaw. "Oh, for Pete's sake! I need hip boots around here. The woods is full of smelly bears and bugling elk. And sorry, it's coyotes eating cats. Besides, who is this 'they,' anyway?"

"Oh, don't be so close-minded. A few years ago, everybody thought wolves were wiped out in Oregon. Then Gordy, the trapper, followed one up in the Wallowas. You never know what's possible."

"Well, if there is one, I hope they don't eat humans. Where I pick pine cones for the Forest Service, it looks like prime Bigfoot country. But I hear humans taste pretty strong. Maybe he'd take one bite and spit me out."

"Who says it's a he? Could be a she. And let's hope she's vegetarian; it's more ethical anyway. Could you please pass the turkey?"

Honest to God, our talks were so goofy and tangential, Gramma Dorothy recorded them for our giggles on quiet, rainy evenings. She even spun these twists into her own Yeti yarn. Just ask if you'd like a copy. An internet blogger nicknamed Rip Jagger, who, I swear, must be a cousin, aptly termed this line of thinking "April Fool's Day all year long."

Just as Bigfoot wandered out of our lives into that deep, dark wilderness whence he came, he popped up again – this time in Gramma's living room. A guest confessed to filming a Hollywood movie called "Sasquatch: The Legend of Bigfoot." It's billed as, "The incredible story of seven men who defied death in a primitive wilderness where no man had gone before... and survived to tell the shocking story of this legendary creature!" Hot stuff! For our giggling grandma, the cinematographer John Fabian signed a movie poster the size of a door – of a hulking Sasquatch silhouette.

What a hoot, but where to hang it? Should you pin Wildman next to Gramma's pressed flowers and an oil painting of Mt. Hood? Maybe that would soften his image. But the only bare spot for the poster is alongside the bathroom. Imagine making a midnight trek to the bathroom, when bleary- eyed, you run into a skulking Sasquatch? Truly, on a dark and stormy night that would be enough to scare the Hyde off Dr. Jekyll.

Revelation
By Janice Strupp

I remember being shocked to not only see Mike smoking, but to see him so deeply inside himself. He was so in the moment, so focused, so contemplative, so unlike my brother. He wasn't my brother at that moment; he was a person separate from me and our parents. Up until then I had not thought of him as anyone other then my older sibling.

Yet, coming across him there on the river bank when I was 13 and seeing him so immersed in his fishing jarred my adolescent idea of family and belonging and individualism and personhood and even love. Maybe that was the moment I realized I loved him while being a little afraid of him in his obvious self-containment. I was startled into a near blinding moment of clarity; an epiphany of truth.

He was so content at that moment. He had everything he needed; all else was superfluous. He was a person – no familial titles, no kinship markers, not even friend. He was a being in the raw, belonging only to himself. Somehow I sensed the enormity and implication of that heretofore unrealized occurrence and state of being. I was awe-struck in its presence. And have remained so these past 50 years.

Photo Gallery

My brother Mike and I when he was 16 and I was 13.
Photo courtesy of Janice Strupp.

Holding Hands
By Karen Wickham

We go our many different ways most days, my Sweetie of 15 years and I. Nearly nightly, however, we converge for our sitting appointment, on the couch holding each others hand, watching a Netflick or a favorite nature or science TV offering, programs we both take pleasure in. It is our looked-forward-to routine, our cozy, coming-together connecting, before the day's closing.

In Gary Chapman's landmark best seller, The Five Love Languages, he posits "We all feel loved and express love in highly personal ways." He describes five different styles of communicating love: quality time, words of affirmation, gifts, acts of service and physical touch.

I've identified my primary one; I crave and long for physical touch.

Lately I've noticed myself unobtrusively holding my own hands, whether folded in my lap or behind my back. How curious. Perhaps I've come to unconsciously associate good touch with tenderness support and self-soothing.

We associate holding hands with lovers. We see them viewing the world from a perspective of two. I am reminded that love does not consist of gazing into each others eyes, but in looking outward together in the same direction. When we see those two in a park, on campus, at the beach, in an elevator, we become captured by our own sweet memories... or we tumble into a miasma of longing. Children's games often circle round holding hands and the kids are always laughing.

My friend's adult daughter recently died from a slow, relentless disease. Even when she slipped into unconsciousness, family members never stopped holding her hand. When Dr. Eben Alexander, as he told in his book, Proof of Heaven, fell into a coma, for seven days, close family and friends, seeing him teetering on the edge of death's abyss never let loose of his hand until he opened his eyes.

As I sit here looking out my picture window at the forest of trees, I hold my own hands. It quiets my mind, grounds me in solid connection. Like a meditation, it carries a message from beyond, "You are OK. You've done nothing wrong. You are held in the arms of love. May your fear, pain and sorrow be eased. Be at peace."

Recently I was on a hike with family. I was walking a distance behind my daughter and her husband, married for nearly thirteen years. I noticed they were holding hands, a sweet moment. They were enjoying the natural beauty and each other at the same time. Was it the Indigo Girls who use to sing, "Multiply Life by the Power of Two?" I think of these two lovers, Lance and Kristel, walking in front of me, nurturing two children and giving back to life on so many levels.

Holding hands. We do much of our connecting these days on the Internet, but that doesn't do it for me – no way! Holding hands, a caring touch, spontaneous or intentional, offers refuge from the tempests of life raging around us. Rather than hand-wringing, hand-holding is what just might comfort, support and sustain us. In a world falling apart, I like to think, two hands at a time will help hold us – and it – together.

Groundwaters

Poetry

Poetry

Table of Contents

BUBBLING UP POETRY (Young Writers' Section)

Photo Gallery

"Old Growth" George Ham of Lorane, Oregon.
Photo courtesy of Alice Ford of Veneta, daughter of poet, Jessie (Stinson) Schlaser

Alice Ford

My grandmother was Ida Ham daughter of Andrew Ham and brother to George Ham. I live a short distance from the Ham homestead on which the original house still stands on Ham Road. I retired after 30 years at Fern Ridge Library as Assistant Director and am currently working part time as Business Manager for my husband's construction/handy-man business. For hobbies I enjoy gardening, rock hounding, reading and making jewelry.

Atonement

I knew this day would come;
It's only fair I guess.
Something has been bugging me;
I should get it off my chest.

These woods I hold so dear to heart,
For years I've laid to waste.
Far and wide, high and low,
We cut to suit our taste.

Three log loads all day long,
Got thirty loads one day.
Never paid it too much time,
That's how I earned my pay.

Seems I've aged a bit and weathered some,
And a lot worse for the wear.
Never even got close to rich,
But I don't really care.

The clear cuts will grow back some day,
Should we cut 'em down again?
And should that be a call that's made,
By narrow-minded men?

All things of earth are intertwined,
And man must use to live.
So who should say how much and when,
And who says it's theirs to give?

We need to get this sorted out,
Conflict tenders little good.
So let's cut back on people,
And save a little precious wood.

~ *Michael J. "Hoss" Barker*

Sunny Sunday Zoo

I took my wife to the Zoo one day, one bright and sunny, Sunday day.
Our car, we quickly loaded up and we went on our merry way.
The lines were long and the Sun was hot, and the sweat beaded off our sun
   burned skin.
We held our place in the long, long line, and eventually they let us in.

Off through the maze of the Zoo we went, my wife and I walked hand in hand.
To see the prisoners kept and caged, far, far away from their native land.
The elephants were the first to see, kept in a concrete hole in the ground.
But when I peered into that hole, I was aghast at what I'd found.

Stains of tears from countless years ran like a river, down his rugged, wrinkled face.
He stood in a corner with his head hung low, and when he moved it was a deathly pace.
The Timber Wolf just lay on the ground, in a filthy dug out hole.
His Spirit had long up and went, patiently waiting for his heart and Soul.

The monkeys swung from rung to rung, locked up in their steel cage.
They couldn't disguise the rage in their eyes, as they screamed together in a mad-
   dening rage.
The bison stood in a cloud of flies as they gnawed through his hide with no respite.
The king of the plains reduced to this was a horrible, horrible, sickening sight.

The hippo's seemed lackluster in their concrete pool.
When it dawned on me I paid for this, my God I felt the fool.
The giraffe still held his head up high, it was either that or die.
But in that Sunday sweltering Sun, I saw tears fall from his eye.

The King of Beasts, the lion, had given up his will and pride.
Had he a say in what Fate would bring he would rather have died.
Then came we to the Eagle, and that was the saddest of them all.
A wire cage for a home for life...those bastards had some gall.

Not even half way through the Zoo that day, did my wife and I traverse.
We could not wait for the exit gate, for my freedom I paid them a curse.
Sleep came hard for me that night, I guess there's thing's I just can't see.
Zoo's aren't bad, but they make me sad, and they just ain't quite my cup of tea.

~ *Michael J. "Hoss" Barker*

Elderly Klamath Falls Man

He shuffles on.

Burnished burgundy pants.
His tired legs limp across hard, unforgiving pavement.
Painfully, each step brings him closer to journey's end.

His tattered blue coat reflects years of wear.
Hard work nestles softly on his shoulders.
Fabric's softness shelters gentleness of spirit.

Back crooked and arched.
His soul stands tall.
Long, strong hands.

Silver band wrapped around one finger, a mate to another.
Reminiscences of a happy, young man.

His smile captures dark, honest eyes.
Laughter and love cradled within the folds of his breast.

He shuffles home.

--Melinda Ann Bender

Thunder
(for Scott)

Thunder strikes its vicious bolts;
tears leap down your face.

With old and new love to hold your hand,
courage wheels you.

Blood courses through your veins;
stopping, retreating.

Your breath slow and raspy;
each step more difficult than the first.

Your body strong and young
writhes in pain.

Your slumped back burns hearts;
motionless face quickens tears.

Black blood coursed through your veins;
chemicals and poisons injected to destroy.

You laughed again; you cried again.
New joys, new loves, and new lives.

Your Goliath battle resurrected;
David's courage and strength guide you.

Excalibur in hand, you slay the darkness.
The storms cease, and the thunderbolts burn out.

You laugh again with new joys:
years to come, children to grow, adults to mature.

Grandchildren to hug,
a loved one to grow old.

--Melinda Ann Bender

Oh Big Sky

Oh Big Sky
Are you watching over me
Shall I say...
What I feel is real today
Will they listen to me now
Will it matter anyhow
What shall I do... for my soul

Do you think you are a master
Do you practice what you preach
So you think your way is faster
Tell me...what is it you teach
Do you show us how to love each other
With more feeling everyday
Are you helping anyone
With more feeling... as you say

Oh Inspiration...
Are you watching over me
Shall I say...
What I feel is real today
Will they listen to me now
Will it matter anyhow
What shall I do... for my soul

If you want to start somewhere
Then start by being true
'Cause if you ain't true
Then we'll find somebody new
Now maybe you can help us all
With what it is you preach
But please don't say you know it all
There's always more to teach

Oh Big Sky
Are you watching over me
Shall I say...
What I feel is real today
Will they listen to me now
Will it matter anyhow
What shall I do... for my soul

~ *C. Steven Blue*

Dragon On You

Am I just dragon on you
Or do you even care
Do you like what I can do
Or do you want to leave my lair

Your silky white hair shines
Hot fire in the sun
The waves of flames it sparks in me
Can cook the heart well done

So claim me
Lady . . . retain me
Just refrain from telling lies

If you just want to brand me
And not stand by me
I'll just fly off in my skies

And burn everything I find!

Am I just dragon on you
Is your love a facade
If you don't want to free me
Don't say a word, just nod

Your woundings, deep as sin
Have bled me till I can't think
They really have sunk in
Even my fiery eyes are pink

So claim me
My queen . . . retain me
But just refrain from telling lies

If you can't stand me
Or command me
I'll just fly off in my skies

And burn everything I find!

I'm a flaming . . . funky . . . scaly
Flying machine

I can be a roaring terror
Or the best mate you've ever seen

I soar the vast blue heavens
Like a lightning rod I pass
I can save you...
Or just grill you
'Cause I'm filled with vigor and sass

But if I'm just a-dragon on you
I'll dismally take my leave
I'll find myself a new dark cave
Where I can flame and grieve

Sorrow is what I'll live by
But I'll find myself again
This hellish pain is hard to swallow
But my fierce roaring fire will win

Hope is all you will have
Inlined with your faith and grace
The only things . . .
Except my wings
That can take you to a higher place

But, if you don't want to . . .
Fly with me
Then so long, my queen
Go, already . . . and find your peace
Before my wrath is seen

Claim me . . .
My queen . . . retain me
But just refrain from telling lies

If you can't stand me
Or command me
I'll just fly off in my skies

And burn everything I find!

~ *C. Steven Blue*

A Day in the Shade

A bee and a flea were having tea on my knee.
"Oh, my," said the fly, who came by to spy.
"May I stay?" asked the fly as she came their way.
"Yes, please," said the bee, handing her some tea.
"How's your daughter, Kate?" asked the flea.
"Kate?" replied the fly. "Kate's great!"
"I hear she has a date," stated the bee, sipping her tea.
"Yes," replied the fly. "Kate has a date with Nate."
The bee leaned forward and quietly said," I hear he's a spider."
"Oh, dear," gasped the flea who sat right beside her.
The fly set down her cup and let out a great sigh.
"I did not know," she said as she got up to go.
"She knows she should only date boys with wings."
The bee said, "Perhaps it's just one of those things.'

"Yes," answered the flea.
"It's just a spring fling."
"Oh, my," sighed the fly.
"Why, oh, why?"
The fly cried, "I would never
see that kind of guy!"
The bee and the flea smiled at each
other and sipped their tea.
"Remember a boy named Troy?
He did not have wings."
"Yes," replied the fly, "but that boy
could sing."
The fly looked toward the sky with a
smile and a sigh.
"I guess we all have a season
for no reason."
The fly gave them each a pat.
"Thanks for the tea and the chat.
"I think it's time I flew. I'm making a stew for Hugh."
"Join us again some time, dear fly," said the bee with a grin.
"Yes," nodded the flea, who was happy to agree.
And, without a sound, the fly flew high above the ground.
Leaving the bee and the flea to finish their tea on my knee

~ Denise Bluth

The Sculptor

I envy a child with eyes of new.
Who does not see life the way I do.
With every experience being his first.
While I must live with an angry thirst,
To wish for death, to start over again,
And not think of how I could have been...
     ...how I should have been.

    We are alone in a simple world.
    It is one of sand and one of pearl.
    A clay figure that we all must shape.
    One I hated and over I did drape,
    A black sheet of ignorant mistrust
    An old tattered cloth of want and lust...
        ...of need and must.

        I envy the wise man with untainted mind.
        Who knows the cold truth is so hard to find.
        REALITY IS NOT PARADISE
        And now it is us who pay the price.
        For all that we know makes what we are.
        The Truth: The future may seem too far...
          ...but the future is what we are

~ *Denise Bluth*

Your Local Symphony Orchestra Plays a Free Show Underneath the Stars

The newspaper today was a
total bummer. Three people were
shot in a movie theater in Pennsylvania.
The weather's supposed to break
100 by Tuesday. More people killed
in some Middle Eastern
country I forget the name of.
Homeless veterans being
displaced from their camp underneath
the bridge. The crossword puzzle was just
impossible. And the library's going to
have to cut back its hours soon.
Things in the world may suck, but they
don't suck tonight. Tonight we get the theme
song from Raiders of the Lost Ark.

~ Kris Bluth

Loophole

It's the 21st century
and she's walking across
the quad listening to a
bootleg of the Dead
on her little
white headphones. Does
it still count as
nostalgia if it was
already old before
you were born?

~ Kris Bluth

A Logger's Last Request

When my time on earth is through and it's my time to go
Lay me down in the forest where the fir and cedars grow
Find a quiet spot, near a clear cut is just fine
I'll watch the reprod grow as I pass the time.

Plant a seedling on my grave, I'll give it a good start
This timberland is dear to me, so place it on my heart
I'll return a little something to this land that gave to me
When its roots begin to grow, I'll become part of that tree

My spirit will be gone. Where? I do not know
Somewhere beyond the stars, that is what I'm told
Perhaps, one day I'll get a glimpse of who I used to be
Growing in the branches of that sacred tree

I'll remember the years I spent working in the woods
Every cherished memory is nothing but good
I'll recall the sounds and scents of a logger's life
Breathe in the smell of sawdust and travel back in time

I'll remember when I cut those tress and laid them down to rest
Just like God in heaven, we only took the best
I miss the guys I worked with, they were a motley crew
But you knew in a pinch they had your back for you

I loved to hear the yarder, let those whistles blow
Bring in another turn and let those chokers go
Out here in God's country, what a life I led
A hard day's work completed when I laid down my head

So, lay me down to rest somewhere in the woods
Plant a tree on me where I can do some good
Don't grieve over me, somehow I will continue on
Though our time on earth is through we're never really gone.

Our presence on this earth might be erased over time
But we live on in the hearts of those we leave behind
Life is ever-changing and if you should miss me
Take a walk out in the woods, I'll be part of God's country.

~ Kala Cota

Small Town Life Back in the Day - Vernonia

A green steel bridge at a curve in the road
Old train trestles that no longer support a load
Shadows of where train tracks used to be
If you come to our town, that's what you'll see

A quiet little valley, set back in the woods
Our memories from here are nothing but good
The lake we enjoy, once, the mill pond
Remnants of mill buildings, others long gone

If you listen real close, you can still hear the whistles
Blowing in the breeze with the cattails and thistles
A long ago time, when a paycheck was earned
Hard work was the lesson that everyone learned

Those old pioneers, they have memories galore
Of tough times and tough men and so much more
They came to this town, set up in the hills
Looking for work and their pockets to fill

To raise a fine family and put food on the table
They were grateful for work and more than able
From dawn until dusk, they worked side by side
An honest day's work was completed with pride

Off at a run when that whistle would sound
Some headed for home, others to town
There were bars, cafés and pretty girls too
For a young man, on the town, there was plenty to do

They built a nice school for all to enjoy
A place to succeed for each girl and boy
Churches were built, prayer was a must
When times got hard, or things went bust

When winter came around and the snow, too
They hunkered down as the cold wind blew
The wood box was filled and lanterns were lit
Around the wood stove, they would all sit

Stories were retold and books were reread
They were early to rise and early to bed
Elk steak, venison, and smokehouse ham
Homemade bread and butter with blackberry jam

There is nothing like life in a small town
Your family and friends all gathered around
No one goes hungry, everyone shares
You'll find in a small town, everyone cares

The simple things in life, they knew their worth
Weddings, baptisms, and a newborn's birth
Celebrations and funerals and a strong belief
That you were never alone in your time of grief

There's a lot to be said for the small town life
Happiness could be found with your children and wife
They took the time to have their share of fun
Good times were waiting when the work was done

They laughed and they joked and horsed around
With a ball and a stick, a game could be found
Picnics and dances, and a small town parade
If you think about it, they had it made!

A bridge, a trestle, trains tracks, and a pond
In our little town the memories live on
Our town in the woods has a proud history
Those brave pioneers left us a great legacy.

~ Kala Cota

Vernonia, South Park and Sunset Steam Railroad excursion crossing the Tophill
or Horseshoe Trestle, Vernonia, Oregon. Courtesy of the Washington County Museum.

parchment

towards the last days, hands hovering
over the smooth white sheets,
the skin seemed like gossamer paper,
leaves of delicate parchment
the color of old pearl, pale and transparent
cool to the touch despite the blood and blue veins
in streaks along the thin wrists,
the thick yellow callouses long abandoned

I feel like I am eavesdropping here
reading a faint calendar of events etched
by broken lines and occasional scars,
your stubborn stigmata, a testimony, silent now
except for your delicate fingers reaching out towards me
tracing the furrowed lines on my hands with
the finality of grace, as if to bid me adieu,
a slight tremble to the touch, granting me a pardon of flesh

as if to remember the caresses and prayers,
remembering the filaments of the past,
the faint fingerprints of age and involvement,
spreading the clean white sheets,
smoothing away the time, ready for salvation,
ready for the sweetness of sleep.

~ Bill Crutchfield

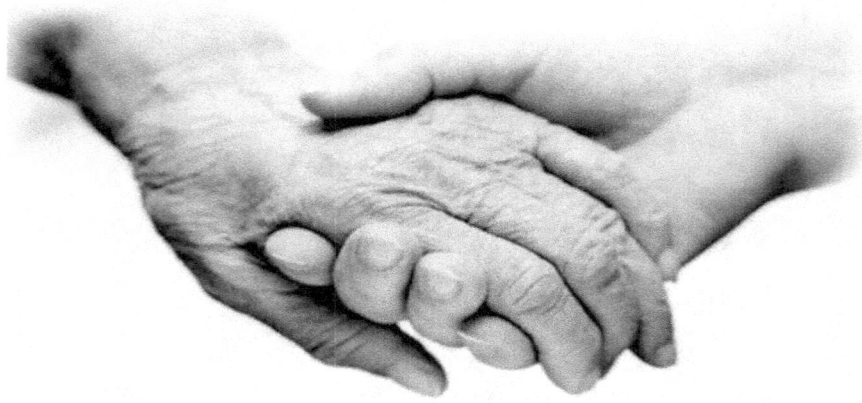

looking up

walking hand in hand, in silence
in the night time hush that briefly surrounds a town
we followed the ancient canal leading us away,
away from the sounds and lights and sights
bundled up in the cloak of winter fog at night

we were warm together, wrapped
in the heavy air, a moistness weighing down
upon us, the fragrant damp woolens pulled close
across our shoulders, almost covering our lips
as if to hush the whispers, our secrets just confessed
in the trembling rose colored blush of exploring love

our breath hung there against the mist,
 visible in the space before us, before the force
of gravity would take its toll, dissolving our speech,
leaving a hole in the night sky,

and suddenly there it was, just a small clearing
of brilliant darkness, and inside, the brief glimpse of a star,
or perhaps an entire constellation, a swirl of dust, or spark,
the tail of Lepus, or the wing of Columba, or perhaps
 magnificent Rigel at the foot of Orion, beckoning,
and I remember saying " look up" then walking on
within that beautiful immersion of silence,
and we could see our whispers floating away,
folding themselves up into the night sky

lost in the darkness, ascending so slowly,
reaching up into the fog, yearning,
becoming a part of the dust
and dissolving into the light.

~ *Bill Crutchfield*

The Music

The music's beauty invades
my heart, my head, and my soul,
with its rush of sound
enveloping my senses.

The driving strength of drum
and pulsing beat of bass viol
partners my own heartbeat
with its own reacting rhythm.

An artist at the piano follows
no visible score but hears or feels
melody as new and as old as life,
but reborn in his hands this day.

From where does music come?
The sigh of wind in trees,
the twitter of birds to their young,
or the soft murmurs of lover's voice.

Born not in croon of clarinet,
nor vibrating strings of violin.
Music is always just waiting
to be captured in someone's mind.

~ Gus Daum

August 11th

She phoned from work,
quiet office voice,

"Hey, Pops, lunch today?
I've got thirty minutes.
Taco Bell okay?"

We met at twelve,
talked about her work,
her kids, my back.

Neither of us mentioned
today's wedding anniversary,
would have been the sixty-ninth.

We did not speak of her mother,
who was in my daughter's eyes,
and whose hand may have
softly brushed my shoulder.

~ Gus Daum

Love

Love is something you share
A feeling with another person.
I am dying today
But, not alone.

She has always been there
"Do you need a drink?"
"I'll take you to the doctor."

She is precious
With that warm smile upon her face.
I've never wanted
To be with anybody else.

As my lights grow dimmer,
I don't need to see.
She makes me feel her affection
And the glory of it all.

She is everywhere she is supposed to be
Helping, caring and loving.
How very fortunate to have
Someone like that in my life.

~ Bob Geller

Bob was the author of "The Sea Remembers All," published in *Groundwaters*, (Volume 9 Issue 2, January 2014). This poem was written one month before his passing.

Living Without You
(In memory of Robert "Bob" Geller)

I can't believe the emptiness I feel
The house is empty without you
How my heart yearns.

To know you are gone
Gone out to the ocean
Gone like a warm spring day.

The nights are long and lonely
My arms go to reach for you
And there is no one to hold.

I miss you.
I miss telling you
"Good morning" and "I love you."

Each day I go forward.
Each day I get out of bed
And get dressed.

The pain, the searing soul sadness
Weighs heavily.
It would be so easy
Just to stay and lie and cry.

But, doing nothing
Doesn't heal me
Doesn't erase the fact you are gone.

My life and living life goes on.
So with tears in my eyes
And sorrow in my heart,
I move slowly, ever slowly, onward
Living without you is
The hardest thing
I've ever had to do.

~ *Katherine Geller*

The Oregon Country Fair

Was at the fair today,
welcomed by joie de vivre
smiling faces and joyful utterances
Mud people in thongs
and naked bottoms
wiggled in procession
to the beat of the drums

With flowing hair and skirts,
girls with painted breasts
sashayed in the aisles
tambourines and ankle bells
lending sound to the smoky drifts
of hemp in the still air

I bought a beautiful mask
of red leather and white feathers
and wore it, pranced along with the crowd
in a belly dance rhythm,
the feathers bobbing in sync
with my happy feet

Today, I found my youth again
and clapped and skipped
with the joy of living.
All that I missed was You,
so that I might also have
the Joy of Loving.

~ Delina Greyling Westling

Landscapes of Our Minds

wispy fingers of mist cling
and creep along the contours of the land
like my intuition fingering along
the dales and moss-covered slopes
of your being ...
oh so gently and gingerly
for your safety and mine

past landscapes have seared me
land mines exploded when
an unwary foot trustingly
stepped on seemingly safe terrain
so I falter sometimes,
with what looks like hesitancy

I know my touch has been invited
yet preservation instincts raise
their voices at times,
motioning Slow Down ...
Speed Zone Ahead ...
Proceed with Caution !

But the child within,
Dorothy with her red shoes,
is Intrepid, Bold, and a Believer ...
with firm hands she is pushing at my back,
her voice whispering in my ear ...
Find out What Can Be,
so it doesn't become, Could Have Been.

~ Delina Greyling Westling

Morgan Station

Morgan Rogue is our grand-niece. Midwives listened to her heart beat during birth. Each time, she sounded so strong, like a train coming; I was inspired to write a poem:

Heartbeat like a train
       bearing down on its destination

Long cry of the engine
       and chugging, chugging, chugging

While those who came to meet her anticipate,
       waiting for the moment when they see her
       coming round the bend

First, we hear her.

The tracks are vibrating.
       Can't quite tell how far away yet
The excitement continues

And then we see the steam!
       Hearing chug, chug, chug, chug, chug...

The lulling crowd gathers tightly
Pressure.

We've been waiting for so long for this day
       for these moments, this life event.

The scouts come running
       shouting what they spied.

Squirrels play in nearby trees.

Time stretches
       while no one is watching the clock

She's been traveling from so far
　　　　another world from here

Everyone strains to see
　　　　the first glimpse
and then the full view

Her tenders are ready

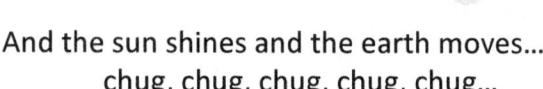

And the sun shines and the earth moves...
　　　　chug, chug, chug, chug, chug...

Love is here. Incarnate.

The light is changing;
　　　　everything seems brighter.

Hearts begin to sing
　　　　and pound, pound, pound...
　　　　beats become one, all one
　　　　wheels on the tracks
　　　　chug, chug, chug

Into the station, into hands, arms,
　　　　embracing, murmuring
home, home, home
　　　　before words, before breath
　　　　Now.

But, no, she slows before arrival.
　　　　Chug, chug, chug; engine crying
　　　　drawing out this moment
　　　　stretching, stretching
before sliding into berth

The engine is pushing, pushing into place

Then she's here! Here!

~ Judy Hays-Eberts

A Splotch of Red

A splotch of red
bobbing in the distance
too far to discern clearly
a funky hat or painted hair I presume
fashionable in this neighborhood
I am curious

A young father takes shape
daughter high on shoulders
little arms clasped tightly round his forehead
ankles firmly in grasp
Orphan Annie hair
bouncing down the sidewalk
chattering away
unabashedly engaged
oblivious to time
or place
or circumstance

Dormant shadows awaken
laughter bubbles out
unexpected tears leak through my mustache
sweet melancholy enfolds me
I glance at the mirror
smile ruefully
and cling to the memory
for just a while longer

tiffanylord

~ *Marv Himmel*

Convulsion

Convulsion in the air tonight
tremors in the hills
rising tide engulfing
time to pay the bills

Serpent stirs from dreaming
about to shed his skin
sleeping gods are waking
chaos dribbles in

Pandora's picked her lock box
Trickster's on the loose
Genie broke her bottle top
Raven flew the coop

Restless growing hunger
anger running deep
time to pay the piper
neglected ways to reap

Too long, too few, too many
cauldron is abubble
change is on the warming wind
Oh are we in trouble

~ Marv Himmel

Return to Yachats #1

It is important to sail
like Yachats' gulls.
Nothing stops their stepping
over outreached piers.

The diverse audience of
boys and girls, under the age of ten
sweep the extensive molten rocks
surrounding the weed and pier.

But the white bearded audience tackles
the gulls' original sounds.
Music from nature, however
is not the control and capture of electronic notes.

~ *Roy Kahn Johnston*

Return to Yachats #2

Arching roofs from land
like ocean spray against rocks,
the town of Yachats
reflects its steep hills
with the crashing waves on its shore..

It is here that we find
a cedar house with sunlit sails of glass
and design of an Asian nation.
The beauty of its diverse gardens,
colors of green, blue, yellow and orange,
reach out and invite us in.

Looking out from the three leveled house
through tree tops toward the shore,
the ocean dances
across the rooftops of the town.

~ *Roy Kahn Johnston*

Today

Be a rainbow in someone's life
Or life-raft on a sinking ship
Be the gentle word that dissipates wrath
Or the water glass on a long dry trip

Be the silver lining on a cloud
Or needle to all the splinters
Be a win in the long string of losses
Or the fire warm in the deep long winter

Be the yes in a life of no's
Or the lighthouse midst the storm
Be the hug in the file of rejections
Or the hiding place through the stinging swarm

So I promise you this, on this very day,
Someone you meet will need what you give
To make it through the rain

~ Keith Kessler

A Goddess

There she stands...a goddess
portal to our temples, our harbors...
seen from great distance, she opens herself, as a satisfied lover...
ships are guided by her luminous jeweled crown.
with lighted torch, she guides their way into the holy of holies..
a new country, a new land... a refuge.
in constant vigil with no guards at her side
she is always vulnerable to throngs of trespassers.
abruptly passing through her, she opens for more.
the tired, the hungry, the poor
welcoming strangers
she welcomes them home.

~ Barbara Newman

Four Black Crows

At water's edge I had prayed
When slicing like black blades
Of ebony on twilight shade
Came the four black crows.

From east to west their way,
Had they sought me all the day?
Had they heard what I had prayed?
What purpose, these four black crows?

I pondered things within my soul
And solemnly wondered at the role
That I had played, and the toll
When they circled, the four black crows.

Around about, above my head
Like veiled priests above the dead
Whose last rites have been read,
Flew the four black crows.

"By lakeside we find the fool!"
Came a voice, thin and cruel;
Their eyes were blackened pools,
Then spoke, the four black crows.

"I am Solitude, thy heart's desire,
A quiet and consuming fire
Holding faster than thickest mire."
Whispered the plainest crow.

"'Tis not the light of God I shun
Nor the joys of rising sun,
But my race is solitary run"
Proudly whispered the plainest crow.

"And me you know on sight,
I am Sin that slinks by night,
Who'll not be overcome by might."
Spoke the blackest of the crows.

"How dreadfully, painfully amusing
The measure of faith you are losing
Is by your own faithless choosing"
Quipped the fairest, blackest crow.

"I am Shame, I've marked thee well,
My roost is in the deepest well
And I am known in blackest Hell."
Said he, the loudest crow.

"It is I who fends off sleep
And have vowed to always keep
Dredging memories from the deep"
Said he, loudest of the crows.

With hands covering o'er my ears
And heart flooded full with tears,
I felt I were a hundred years
And so queried the four black crows.

"Tell me now, you vile four
Who speaks next above lakeshore?
Who remains to condemn once more?
And who dispatched you four crows?"

"For my crimes, shall I be lost?
To be redeemed, what is the cost?
Was it Heaven or Hell you crossed
To scourge me now, you four black crows?"

"Of these four I am the last,
Beneath my shadow art thou cast,
Self-condemned by sinful past."
Spoke aloud, the largest crow.

"I am he that tarries yet,
Whom your soul shall not forget;
Eternally yours, I am Regret."
Assuredly spoke the largest crow.

"Solitude may be repaired,
Sin is progeny of despair,
And Shame will die, as Christ is fair"
Preached he, the largest crow.

"But, you surely know that I endure,
I am rare, an emotion pure,
For this cancer, there'll be no cure"
Boasted aloud the last of crows.

"You'll be forgiven and then find
That all is never quite left behind
And keen memory can be unkind"
Reminded me, the final crow.

"Mark these words I speak to thee,
That in your soul I'll always be,
From my embrace, you're never free."
Vowed the last, undying crow.

~ *Brian Palmer*

. . . .

Frolicking

Jays squawking loudly,
Children playing in the park,
Serenity broken.

The Haiku

Just five syllables
Seven more is suitable
Finished off with five.

~ *Jim Miller*

Leroy's Christmas Eve

It was Christmas Eve
And all over the spread
There was nary a sound,
Most all were in bed

Rufus was a-snorin'
By the fire in Long-Johns,
Bubba sippin' egg-nog
Out back in the john

Cleotus with needle and thread
Was mending his old britches,
And Leroy was scratchin'
Back where it itches

I was reading the classics
A tale of pain and hate,
Batman versus the Riddler
Issue number 338

When something came to Leroy,
It pert near resembled a thought,
"Hey, lissen here fellas,
Is ol' Santy dead or not?"

I fell backwards outta my chair
Landed square on my butt,
Cleotus gouged hisself and hollered,
"You some kind of dad-gummed nut?!"

Rufus bolted straight upright,
Eyeballs blinking wide awake,
"Leroy, that there's sackfiligeous
For goodness sake!"

I scrambled up from the floor
With my classic of hate and pain,
"Son," I blurted out,
"What's wrong with your pea-brain?"

"Shoot fellas, I'm just askin',
I ain't saying that he is,
I just got to thinking
Well, you know, gee whiz!

I ain't never really seen him
All up-close like
Since he left that beef jerky
With my red pedal trike

He looked a hunert then
With that white beard an' all,
And what about them body doubles
Working at the mall?"

'Ol Leroy looked pure serious,
I could see it in his face
Rufus said, "Well, askin' questions
Ain't no disgrace"

We set down at the folding table
And put the coffee on,
I figured we'd settle this
If it took us all 'till dawn

Leroy looked at all of us
Like it was the Inquisition,
Cleotus cleared his throat,
"This here's the sityation"

"Santy Clause don't age at all
He's always been an ol' Cuss,
When he first lassoed them reindeer
He was older than all of us!"

"That's right" Rufus said
Pouring coffee in his cup,
"Why, don't you know 'ol Santy
Ain't never been a young pup?"

"Yessir," I sat up and said
Puttin' in my two cents,
"He was older than the hills
'Afore they had bob-wire fence"

We were nodding at Leroy
Reassuring our worried friend,
When a crash shook the bunkhouse
From front to back end!

The back door burst open
And there in the night,
A giant of a man
Who looked ready to fight!

He had a big barrell chest
And ham-sized fists,
Spurs on his boots
And a beard white as snow drifts

With a boom he bellowed,
"Somebody find 'ol Leroy
Tell him get outside,
I brung some things for the boy!"

We all gulped real hard
Leroy stood from the table,
He walked out the front door
Though he was barely able

The stranger wore a hat
Atop his stark-white hair,
He spit in the fire
And pulled up Leroy's chair

Under that big floppy hat
Was a pair of blue eyes
Bright, happy, bigger than Dallas
Yessir, they were Bubba-size!

He pulled down his fake beard
And gave a big wink,
"Now lissen up fellas
Here's what Leroy'll think

That Santy's been awful busy
With a million other youngsters
Handin' out video games
And antique Herman Munsters"

Just then Leroy hollered out,
"Come out here boys, hurry up
Before he hits the trail,
Quick, he's saddlin' up!"

Bubba, Cleotus, Rufus and I
Gawked at one another
Leroy yelled, "Lookit that sleigh,
You won't believe that mother!"

We spilt from the bunkhouse
And fell all over ourselves,
Stomped on mustaches and eyebrows
Like four big, stupid elves

We crawled through the door
And out into the snow,
Leroy was yellin',
"Man, lookit him go!"

He was pointing high
At a glorious sight
Hoss, I won't soon forget
That Christmas Eve night!

There in the powdery snow
Laying all around our feet
Were pocket knives, spare bullets,
Cowboy hats, all kinds of treats!

Wrist watches, wool socks,
Turkey calls and new boots,
And a brand-spankin' new
Sunday go-to-meetin' suit!

And right in the middle
Of the whole dad-gum mess,
Leroy was holding up
A pink flowery dress

"He said this is for ma,
She sold the one she had
When she needed the cash
For bail money for dad!"

We were all just blinking
For certain out of breath,
I knew I wasn't dreaming
I was scared to death

Bubba was a-stutterin',
"But...but...but I...."
Leroy said, "Shoot, I never knew
Clydesdales and mules could fly!"

~ *Brian Palmer*

The Porch

They came from the South,
Like soldiers,
Marching, destroying,
Leaving nothing in their wake.

We heard
They were coming,
A temporary annoyance,
Not cruel.

But standing on that porch,
The dog whining,
I heard awful rumbles,
Pounding and swelling.

Blacky slipped under the couch.
I struck my shin
On the way to the TV,
No picture.

Back on the porch,
I looked around.
Martha yelled "Run!"
Then slammed her door.

I dialed Lester,
The line was dead,
Then decided to climb,
Grabbing a ladder.

Propped against my porch roof,
I shoved the dog up,
Then pulled myself up top
By the wisteria.

From the roof
I watched them coming,
The waves, the water,
And I wept.

Miss Charlotte floated by,
Clinging to an old tire,
Sputtering and coughing.
I shouted and waved.

She disappeared.
I sobbed and prayed.

Lester came.
I didn't know we'd
Ever see each other again.
We are lucky.

The wallpaper still shows
High water marks,
But not all we've lost --
Seven people in our parish.

No porch,
I drag my rocker outside.
Martha waves.
We cry, then laugh.

It's springtime.
Where my porch once stood,
The gnarled wisteria
Still twines.

Rachel Rich

Spider Work of Art

As I sit staring out of the window – a
daily habit – a tiny spider
Weaves a deadly web
of deceit. The wind blows her back and forth.

Undeterred, she continues to form what?
From this distance it looks invisible.

My attention is drawn to more urgent,
and important events.
Trees waving their
Branches in the wind, cloud formations
and an approaching rain squall.

Soon the tiny spider appears to be asleep –
in the center of her deadly trap.

~ Doug Russell

Fern Ridge Egrets

Eight Egrets, dressed in priestly white,
Stand very still along mud flats and
shallow water lines waiting
for this morning's sacrificial offering.

Their white a contrast against
the muddy waters and blue skies –
White the color for purity.
Their motives are not priestly nor pure.
Silent, still and waiting, they are driven
by one need, one instinct –
Hunger.

They have no emotion, compassion, or mercy
But, they are a part
of this wonderful, beautiful
world we live in.
Do you understand –
this is the real world?

I'm not trying to pass a judgment
Or put this into a box, tied with a neat pretty ribbon.
I'm just saying, a small school of fish and some frogs,
Whom are also part of this wonderful world
Are taking their last swim.

~ *Doug Russell*

A Dog's Prayer

Treat me kindly, my beloved master, for no heart in the world is more
grateful for kindness than the loving heart of me.
Do not break my spirit with a stick, for though I lick your hand
between blows, your patience and understanding will more quickly
teach me the things you would have me do.

Speak to me often, for your voice is the world's sweetest music,
as you must know by the fierce wagging of my tail when
your footstep falls upon my waiting ear.

When it is cold and wet, please take me inside, for I am now
a domesticated animal, no longer used to bitter elements.
And I ask no greater glory than the privilege
of sitting at your feet beside the hearth.
Though had you no home, I would rather follow you through ice and snow
than rest upon the softest pillow in the warmest home in all the land,
for you are my god, and I am your devoted worshiper.

Keep my pan filled with fresh water, for although I should not reproach you
were it dry, I cannot tell you when I suffer thirst.
Feed me clean food, that I may be well, to romp and play
and do your bidding, to walk by your side, and stand
ready, willing and able to protect you with my life should your life
be in danger.

And, beloved master, should the Great Master see fit to deprive me
of my health or sight, do not tum me away from you.
Rather, hold me gently in your arms as skilled hands grant me the merciful
boon of eternal rest... and I will leave you, knowing,
with the last breath I drew,
my fate was ever safest in your hands.

~ *Jessie Stinson*

Soccer

If I had played soccer when I was a girl
I'd have deftly dodged the antics of
my three brothers
when necessary.
I'd have learned teamwork
and known when to kick a pass and
when to keep the ball to myself.
I'd have learned it's okay to use your
elbows now and then and,
although sometimes a goal is reached
with giant running strides,
more often it is done with short quick steps and
adeptly maneuvered footwork.
I'd have been like my granddaughter's
team flowing like sanderlings following
the outgoing waves on the beach
and then running back
with the incoming foam.
I'd have learned that it's not a disaster to fall down;
that it's good to reach a hand out to a fallen team member;
and that you can't always win but
you can always try to examine your game
and do better the next time.
I'd have known that my body was capable
of more than I knew when I started
and that a tough sport
can build confidence and friendships
as well as muscles.
I'd have learned that if you are not
enjoying it
you can find a different game to play,
one that you love.
If I had played soccer when I was a girl
I would have known all this much
sooner.

~ *Susanne Twight-Alexander*

Bunchberry Dogwood

Do you remember the bright red drupe
on the bunchberry,
the little plant no more
than five inches high?
It was perched among ferns
on a rocky shelf facing Maidenhair Fall,
right by the bridge.
All the other berries in that cluster
were gone.
This one remained – shiny, sturdy,
witness to the wonder of
falling water and rushing stream,
witness to the few birds
of the old growth forest
and the fox that comes to drink
at the creek's edge,
witness to the dipper
that nests in its spray
below the bridge
where shaded gorge
steers noisy flow.
We paused to admire
the waterfall
but who noticed the small plant?
Who would guess that,
in the spring, white bracts
with tiny greenish flowers will appear,
centered,
just like its much larger cousin, the dogwood tree.
I'm sure the bunchberry
did not mind this neglect.
It was focused on something
more enduring.

~ *Susanne Twight-Alexander*

Rebels

Some people burn
wake up on fire
are maddened
at the simplicity
of their day jobs
are discouraged
with the ease
of their wives
these people are
not average
or easily amused
they tend to blow
up their televisions
and rage at
the news
pray to
the stars
the sun
they are
the mad ones
the outcasts
the addicts
the cowboys
artists
the free souls for
whom daily living
is hard
life is too
mundane for
those who
wake up on fire

~ Terah Van Dusen

Poetry vs Love

When I love
I am not a poet but
a homey thing in an
apron with dreams
in my eyes with hands
too wet to write

When I fall or
am pushed out of love
I am a poet again
wet eyes
dry hands
words flying from my
fingertips like the children
I had hoped to bear with him

Sometimes I wonder if
I am destined for poetry
and not love
more and more I fear
they cannot, will not
coexist

~ *Terah Van Dusen*

The Poets...

despairing of ever receiving
a warm cup of adoration from an ice-fisted world,
decided to try their collective hands at suicide.

one unfortunate
leapt from a shallow curb into
a lazy rivulet of soapy off-wash
from a down-street suv's summer bath.
all he got for his trouble was
a matching pair of soaked trouser cuffs.

another
hung himself from a bedroom closet robe-hook
with a noose fashioned from strands of spider saliva.
the only injury sustained was his pride,
as he went bump in the embarassed dark
falling butt-first into a heap of dirty laundry.

one girl,
locking herself in a high-school commode,
played tic-tac-toe on her wrists with
a sharp red crayon.
upon being discovered,
her reward was
to be marched to the school counselor's office
by the vice-principal
and presented as a cautionary tale against
unsanitary body-piercing techniques.

yet another misbegotten soul
planted himself in the direct path of
a grandmother wobbling a shopping bag
on walker wheels.
he emerged from the debacle
boasting only a cracked cuticle upon his left big toe,
and the uneraseable memory of her outraged scowl.

finally,
the poets gave up their tragedian's act
as they slowly came to the realization that

whatever hated portions of liver and spinach
you excuse yourself from the night before
will be served cold for tomorrow's breakfast.

so plug your nose,
swallow hard,
and graciously try to digest
whatever this brutal life throws on your tray.

~ *Erik Wahl*

Photo Gallery

Hop pickers on Doane Road (southeast of Crow, Oregon)

Heaven's Lane

When Time's watch is over, Love covers all.
We flatten our souls on anvils of pain;
Hate makes us stumble; Shame makes us crawl.

How long World's valley, how thick Mind's wall!
What fools call folly, sages count sane;
When Time's watch is over, Love covers all.

Truth's bent and battered in Self's silvered hall,
Sweet Mercy's cream rinsed down Mammon's drain;
Hate makes us stumble; Shame makes us crawl.

We wait half-sleeping Redemption's call;
Stiff-bristled creeds won't lift Adam's stain.
When Time's watch is over, Love covers all.

Love every heart or love not at all;
We make the choice to walk Heaven's lane.
Hate makes us stumble; Shame makes us crawl.

Dance with the angels at Joy's wedding ball!
Clap carefree hands to Mercy's refrain!
When Time's watch is over, Love covers all.
Hate makes us stumble; Shame makes us crawl.

~ Erik Wahl

A Holiday on the Beach

A holiday, conceived and planned.
Four older women, friends, would go to the beach together.

Snippets of excited conversation ensued, emails, phone, face-to-face
To lay out the necessary, complex plan to assure a successful outing

Urgent calls, last minute to secure the final arrangements. The plan:
A walking beach absolutely, a funky dress shop in a quaint geodesic building
Reservations at The Waterfront.

Rations were brought to accommodate every imaginable Portlandia diet
for a midday picnic
Who should drive? Will there be room for chairs? What if it rains?
How long should we stay?

Only one item unfortunately forgotten, begged to be considered:
Each mature sage woman, tucked within her secret soul an eager little girl,
Clapping and jumping up and down. "Finally, this is my playdate at the beach!"

She said "I can't wait to show off my favorite boutique!" No one was impressed.
All impatient to leave.
Looking for the perfect picnic spot, she said,
"I need this sun-splashed bench by the river to soothe my frazzled nerves
from driving.
She said, "I'm sitting at this roomy, rustic shaded table to share
my yummy offerings."
With proud smile, she said, "I brought chocolate, gluten-free cupcakes for each."
She said, "I can't eat sugar."

Upon arriving at the beach, her heart sang,
She said, "Lets race to the water, revel in its awesome energy, wiggle toes in the
surf and say 'hello' to this beloved ocean."
She said, "We've found the perfect spot in the dunes far back from the waves,
Sheltered from the wind."

She said, "We two will take a fast walk along the beach while you two slower
ones watch our stuff.
Half hour passed. Returning breathless, she said, "We need to leave in seven
minutes to catch our reservations at the Waterfront Depot.

Her heart sank. To herself she said, "Now no time to walk on the jetty
and see the bird's view."
She said, "The beach is so much more fun when the sun is shining."
But it wasn't.

She said, she said, she said and she said. . . . .
Alas the day marched onward in its own ordered way.

All the little girls' emotions bled sorrow on the sand, while
Each mature, intentionally flexible adult strove to quiet and comfort the rebuked,
squashed, screaming and sorely disappointed little one inside her.

Four adults, four little girls, all had SO hoped to play!

~ *Karen Wickham*

Photo Gallery

Man and woman cooking hotdogs on the beach at Heceta Head north of
Florence, Oregon, 1938. *Photo by Ralph Gifford; Oregon State Archives, Dept/Trans-
portation, #OHDG485*

"Bubbling Up" Poetry

(From our talented under-18 contributors)

I am a Symphony

I am a symphony
Sometimes soft and mellow
other times rousing and grand
but other times sad and mournful
all of my melodies have their own feelings
their upbeat and happiness
and their mournfulness and sadness

Sometimes they are shy and fearful
but sometimes they are assertive
and rousing
with a strong beat

But all of them
even if they are sad
or upbeat and happy
are beautiful in their own way

For I am a symphony.

~ Abraham Lawrence, age 13

At School

At a school where math
and writing are done
I think about its mysteries
its secrets

~ Abraham Lawrence, age 13

Mountains

Mountains can be forested
with streams like silver snakes
twisting, turning
and curving
down their sides.

Or with rocky ridges
shifting sands
and barren terrain.

Though other mountains are barren
in a magnificent way
their slopes beautifully carved
by the wind
in elegant patterns
and curving ravines.

Or some mountains
are volcanic
and hostile,
a hot and dry rock
red with lava.

Still others just look like a snowy mountain,
but if you think about it,
all mountains are just mountains
even if they look
like a hump-back camel
or a domed church
or a brown lump that from a distance
if you stare at it long enough
resembles a farmer's wife

--it's still just a mountain.

~ Abraham Lawrence, age 13

[in·tro·vert]

[By *Nick-DeAngelo*]

- An autobiographical webcomic about unrequited narcissism.

Nick DeAngelo is a Fern Ridge-bred cartoonist/videographer. Nick is currently living in Eugene's artsy beer-soaked Whiteaker neighborhood. Nick studied graphic design in high school, when he was commissioned to design a masthead and logo for local writers' publication *Groundwaters* (yeah, that was me). This era of Nick's life was documented in his first comic *Just Add Water*. By the time he earned his Associate's degreee in multimedia at LCC, he was doing his follow-up comic, *Greetings From Eugene*. He now works at a local video production company, Stafford Video Productions. Nick is currently documenting his life in his third comic strip installment, [in•tro•vert].

Our Contributors...
angels all

OUR CONTRIBUTORS

Contributors for this Issue

Mary Alexander

Mary spent her childhood in California, Oregon, Arizona and Indiana. Six months after high school graduation she married her Hoosier boyfriend who was then serving in the Air Force. The next twenty plus years she was busy raising their two sons and being a camp follower with multiple assignments in the United States, three years in Japan, and four years in Europe. Upon her husband's retirement Mary returned to college at the University of Arizona. She earned her Bachelor's degree in Psychology and Sociology, plus a Master's degree from Arizona State University in Clinical Social Work.

Her twenty-five years as a social worker included two years in Tucson's school system and five years in Child Protective Services. She then opened her own counseling and psychotherapy practice in Sierra Vista, Arizona for eighteen years. She declares she is now on her "fourth life" as an author of short stories, memoirs, and three books that are pending publication. Her life has given her abundant material for her writing.

. . . .

D.J. Barber

dj barber lives on the western edges of Eugene, Oregon with his lovely wife, Peggy and their two small dogs. His love of reading led to a passion for writing. Working odd days and hours, dj takes time out and writes about fantasy, science fiction, horror, and even detective noir. Time is also well spent in various Willamette Valley vineyards nearby Eugene, Veneta, and Junction City, sipping fine wines, breathing deep, and enjoying the wonderful scenery while his muse sends thoughts his way.

Michael J. "Hoss" Barker

Hoss Barker is a self-proclaimed redneck who spent his younger adult years working in the logging industry in the backwoods of Oregon; he is also a poet in the truest sense of the word.

Hoss took a job at Paradise Lodge on the scenic Rogue River so that he could write his poetry. While there, he published three books of poetry (*Out of Oregon: Logging, Lies and Poetry*, 2003; *The Ballads of Lewis & Clark*, 2004; and *Tin Cups and Horseshoes*, 2008.) *My Time in Paradise*, a full-length memoir published in 2014, is Hoss' story of those six years spent in the wilderness that he loved.

. . . .

Melinda Ann Bender

I grew up in Oregon, was born in Seattle, attended the University of Washington, graduated from Oregon State University, and I am a teacher. I love the rain and geography of Oregon and Washington and write from this perspective. My early love of poets originated from classes I took from beloved Oregon Poet Laureate, Paulann Petersen.

. . . .

C. Steven Blue

After a 27 year career in stage production in Hollywood, CA, I currently pursue my lifetime calling as a lyrical/performance poet. I am the publisher/managing editor of Arrowcloud Press and producer and host of local poetry events, including The Poetry Stage @ Festival of Eugene and the annual Poetry Workshop & Poetry Showcase at the Eugene Public Library. I often volunteer my services and performances in support of local causes. I publish other poets and have 4 published books of my own, as well as a blog on my website, http://www.word-songs.com.

Denise Bluth

I am 44 years old and recently married an amazing man, Kris Bluth. We live in Eugene with his nine-year-old daughter, Sammy. I also have two grown sons who are both away at college out of state. I have been writing for as a long as I can remember, but haven't been officially published, because I have a heavy fear of rejection. Kris is really very supportive and insisted I, at least, try.

. . . .

Kris Bluth

Kris Bluth lives in Eugene with his wife Denise and his daughter Sam. When not writing, he enjoys arguing with strangers on the Internet and falling asleep to episodes of Mystery Science Theater 3000. His work has most recently appeared in *Bay Laurel*, *Doves and Serpents*, and *Eugene 150th Birthday Celebration Poetry Celebration*.

. . . .

Stanley Buck

I was born in Astoria, Oregon during a rainstorm in 1934. In 1944, my parents moved to the upper Smith River, near Gunter, a few miles from Drain. I went in the service in 1952, spending 5 years in the Navy, and 19 years in the Air Force. I retired and moved to Waldport, Oregon in 1976.

I graduated from Minot State University in 1974 while in the Air Force, and attended graduate school both in Minot, North Dakota and in Oregon. I was married for 58 years to my sweetheart, Sieglinde, and we had three children. She died last year. Everything I ever did or became I could not have done without her.

Jennifer Chambers

Jennifer Chambers writes about strong women with bold stories. She speaks across the United States about persevering through traumatic brain injury and genetic disorder. Her work has been published in numerous national newspapers, magazines and websites. As a person with cognitive disability, it's important for her to tell stories about real people living extraordinary lives—and, conversely, tell stories about extraordinary people living ordinary lives in her fiction.

. . . .

Larry Chura

Larry Chura was born in Toronto, Canada, but was schooled and educated in the United States. For many years, he went with his parents back to the family homestead in Saskatchewan during the summers. He became a naturalized citizen in 2002 for the second time after his original papers were lost by the INS and he is very proud of that accomplishment.

    He loves animals and is also an avid hiker, but because of health reasons, has had to cut back. Currently he fills his time writing, visiting grandkids and going on short walks.

. . . .

Gene Conrad

My interest in writing evolved by accident. The first story I wrote was for our family Christmas letter. My wife Julie asked me to write something to include. I decided to focus on some goofy thing that had happened. Pat Edwards, editor of *Groundwaters* was on our Christmas letter list and invited me to submit stories for the magazine. The real events that happen to all of us that are crazier than things we can make up... those are the kind of things I enjoy writing about. I write for two reasons: 1) I did not know my grandparents and it is my hope to record a little of my life. My descendants can perhaps get a small glimpse of who I am. 2) I write to encourage others to share their stories with the people they love.

Kala Cota

I live in my hometown of Vernonia, Oregon, with my high school sweetheart, who I married two years after graduation. We have two grown children and a beautiful granddaughter, Avery. I have been teaching preschool in my home for the last 27+ years. I enjoy telling stories in rhyme; in fact, I think in rhyme a lot, which can be very annoying and usually requires a few minutes spent at the computer to get it on paper and out of my head. Writing poems is definitely my creative outlet and therapy at times.

. . . .

Bill Crutchfield

William C. Crutchfield was born in Memphis Tennessee, raised in Fresno, California and earned a degree from the University of Oregon "way back in the early 1980's." He's been a Lane Country resident since 1973 and an Elmira resident since 1999. His philosophy? "Write it as if no one was ever going to read it, but write it."

. . . .

Gus Daum

I'm venturing into my active tenth decade. I've been writing for many years in the business field but now, upon retirement, I am into "fun" writing – including poetry and short fiction.

Presently I am a proud Oregonian for the past 45 years. I was born on a Kansas farm before the Great Depression, saw the Pacific Ocean courtesy of the US Navy in World War II, attended two Kansas universities and have continuing interest in all their athletics, particularly Kansas University where I played basketball in the late mid-forties. Creaking joints have retired me to bicycles and auto's.

I was happily married for sixty-seven years until my spouse's death a year ago. I am blessed with three children – all amazing and all supportive.

Dale R. Dickson

Dale R. Dickson obtained his Electronic Engineering degree from New Mexico State University in 1962. After working in the aerospace industry for three years, he desired a more active occupation and joined the Los Angeles City Fire Department. He gained firefighting experience and was promoted to the rank of Captain. Dale retired after 26 years of active duty and moved to Eugene.

He enjoys writing and his accomplishments include a novel, *Camp Nine*, a story of life in a chain gang in the Jim Crow south, and *Jake the Fire Mouse*, a childrens' story book about a heroic mouse that lives in a firehouse.

His enthusiasm for writing remains strong, and he has had his works published in several magazines including *Good Old Days, Country, History Channel, Reminisce* and *Groundwaters*.

· · · · · · · · · · · · · · · · · ·

Natalie Edwards

Natalie Edwards is 11 years old and is a 6th grader at Creswell Middle School in Creswell. Her Halloween stories included in this book were written when she was in 5th grade, however.

Natalie likes to read and has proven to be a talented writer with a vivid imagination and strong story-telling skills.

She will be playing volleyball at Creswell Middle School for the 2015-16 school year.

· · · · · · · · · · · · · · · · · ·

Pat Edwards

Pat Edwards is an author, editor, publisher and historian. She has written two books on the history of Lorane, Oregon and served as the managing editor and publisher for *Groundwaters* magazine, a literary quarterly which was published and distributed for over 10 years throughout Lane County.

Most recently, Pat has spent over two years working with author Jo-Brew as editor, collaborator, researcher, publisher and co-author of two major books on the history of Highway 99 through Oregon called OREGON'S MAIN STREET: U.S. Highway 99 "The Stories" and "The Folk History," which were published in 2013 and 2014, respectively.

David R.L. Erickson

My wife, Christina & I live in Crow with two cats, a dozen chickens, and a sweet wind-up dog named Angie. I am a CNA2 working in an ambulatory surgery center. I self-published a science fiction western in November of 2013 entitled *White Fist & Two Dogs*, and am working daily on the second of the series.

. . . .

Michael Foster

The author is a retired educator with a bachelor's degree in Elementary Education, a Master's in Special Education with several hundred hours of post-graduate study in Assessment and Systems Performance. Mr. Foster has been married to the same woman for more than forty years, has two children who are both college graduates and are in stable relationships and self-supporting. His children and his six grandchildren are his Wakanisha; family is the most important part of his life. *Wakanisha Is Love Enough* is his first novel.

. . . .

Bob and Katherine Geller

Through my life's mountain, the climb has been very steep. The view, once through the darkness, has been a great light. This has provided a great catalyst to being a voice for those lost, alone and without hope.

Bob and I met 12 years ago; it was those vivid blue. eyes that got me. When he realized he loved me, he was concerned about his age. I said that age is just a number. Thanks, Bob, for 4 wonderful years and taking me to the moon. ~Katherine Geller

Bob's bio in 2013: *"I'm a 75-year-old kid who loves his grandkids and enjoys writing stories. I guess that makes me a storyteller."* He passed away on December 18, 2014.

Dana Graves

If Dana had a motto, it should be, "Don't Fence Me In." Dana has always loved a challenge, finding them with a variety of jobs. He tried his hand at bull riding in a rodeo; he's been a logger in Oregon & Idaho and a construction worker. He worked on an oil rig in Wyoming, at an army depot in Utah, and on the railroad in California. He hiked the Chilkoot Trail, the path of gold seekers of the 1800s and followed a series of jobs in Alaska... fishing, mechanic, and cattle rancher on the islands of Kodiak, Sitkalidak and Sitkinak. He began journaling during the confinement of bad weather and short days and long nights, which later led to his writing poetry.

In his spare time Dana has enjoyed hunting, fishing and flying his plane. He now lives in Stites, Idaho with his wife Paula. During his life, Dana has had some close brushes with death... but he still rushes headlong into life. *(Photo courtesy of Gary Littlefield)*

. . . .

Mildred Thacker Graves

I am a compulsive people-watcher and especially enjoy writing about people I know. I also find pleasure in writing about people I do not know, but only observe and about whom I often speculate. Most of my writing is about and for my family. Of course, friends are not out-of-bounds at times for my reflections. Watch out friends and family! Someone may be watching YOU!

(Photo by Marcia Murphy)

. . . .

Delina Greyling Westling

Delina, born in sunny South Africa, loves primary colors and textures. She paints pictures with words, or with paint, or by sculpting clay ... drawing from childhood experiences among the Ndebele, Xhosa, and Zulu people.

Delina lived in Eugene for several years until 2014 when she moved to the foothills of the Sierras, in California, trekking after the sun ... and now happily gardens on ten acres of chaparral with her hubby, John.

Judy Hays-Eberts

Judy Hays-Eberts is the voice of a soul grounded in Oregon, enlivened by nature, writing as the words flow through. It's meant for encouragement of the heart. Previously published work may be found at www.groundwaters.org.

. . . .

John Henry

Our family moved out to Oregon over thirty years ago. It was love at first sight. The ocean, rivers, mountains, ancient forests, high desert and our glorious Willamette Valley opened us to new, grand possibilities. Some of the possibilities were a return for me to camping, hiking, travel and writing. Antelope, pileated woodpeckers, golden eagles, hot springs, Saturday Market and the annual whale migration are just a few of the Oregon delights that have stimulated the poetry within. Memories of living through the 60s and active service in Vietnam have also moved me to write about my personal experiences, warped by anger, frustration and love.

. . . .

Evelyn Hess

For 15 years, Evelyn Hess and her husband lived in a tent and trailer, without electricity or running water, on 20 acres of wild land in the foothills of the Oregon coast range. When they at last decided to build a real house, they knew it would have to respect the lessons of simple living that they learned in their camping life. With unfailing wit and humor, *Building a Better Nest* chronicles their adventures as they seek a model for sustainable living not just in their home, but beyond its walls. Hess's first book, *To the Woods*, earned a WILLA Literary Award for Creative Nonfiction. Watch a recent short TV interview with Evelyn at http://www.katu.com/amnw/segments/Building-a-Better-Nest-311317851.html. She also appears on http://www.rosecityreader.com

Marv Himmel

I am a member of the writer's group that meets at the Campbell Senior Center in Eugene each Thursday. I have never attempted to publish anything before, but I am retired now and have rekindled a life-long interest in writing that the writer's group helps to nourish.

. . . .

Sherry Hunter

Sherry Hunter aka Grandma Sherry is a retired horse woman who spent her life training horses and ridership, giving clinics and judging horse competitions. She was active in youth work and in retirement has continued to work with children as a volunteer at schools, church and in her neighborhood. She writes children's stories, inspirational and motivational articles and stories for adults, and is presently working on a historical biography. Her stories are full of true life people and adventures from life among animals and the people who love them. (If not actual, she wishes they could be!)

. . . .

Bridgett Johnson-Elliott

Bridgett was born on a peaceful, snowy night 24 years ago. She is blessed to live and work in the beautiful Pacific Northwest, surrounded by loving family and the company of old-growth forests. She enjoys writing stories, playing music and creating art. Bridgett is interested in pursuing the publication of children's books and illustrative art with a focus on animals, nature, and home. Bridgett holds two Associate degrees from Lane Community College in Arts & Languages and furthers her studies at the UO. She has been an active volunteer for many non-profit organizations over the years

Roy Kahn Johnston

Roy Kahn Johnston is an internationally recognized poet who has been published in a wide variety of magazines. His books include *The System is Broken, Seeds of Tolerance, Kenosis; San Luis Obispo, Dissonance and Consonance, The Wandering Circle, From Fractals Forward* and *Steps In Life.* He has been a featured reader at the Annenberg Rare Book and Manuscript Library, University of Pennsylvania; University of the West Indies, Mona, Jamaica; Beyond Baroque, Venice, CA; Peoples' Republic of China, Galaxy II, Yangtze Cruise; Nahargarth Palace, Madhopur, India; Globus Tour, Portugal; Dubrovnik, Croatia, University of Oregon Eugene and Portland campuses, and the San Luis Obispo Poetry Festivals. He has hosted noted poets and authors on his program "Cerebral Meditations", BlogTalkRadio. He holds a doctorate in music from USC, a master's from The Juilliard School and matriculated at the Wiesbaden Conservatory in Germany. He played classical and jazz clarinet, taught, and served as Assistant Dean of Fine Arts at the University of Southern Mississippi and Dean of the Boston Conservatory. He completed the poetry requirements for the USC Master of Professional Writing Program and studied poetry at the Charles University in the Czech Republic and the William Joiner Center for War and Its Social Consequences at the University of Massachusetts, Boston. He was recognized by the California Legislative Assembly and the City of Los Angeles for his 35 years of honorable service as "Performer, Professor, Poet and Pioneer in the field of "cultural integration."

. . . .

Reida Kimmel

I hang on to things. The things I loved as a youngster -- books, the outdoors, gardens, museums, knitting, teddy bears, and most especially horses, are still important seventy years later. Charles Kimmel and I have been married for 53 years and have one married son living in Eugene. I trained as a history teacher, but ended up working in Charles' zebrafish lab for more than 30 years. We live on a little homestead with our horses, sheep, chickens, dogs, cats, and the all too abundant garden. I am devoted to self sufficient and sustainable living, which conflicts philosophically with my love of travel. I enjoy working with the Eugene Natural History Society and Forestland Dwellers, both groups devoted in their different ways to science education.

Keith Kessler

Keith Kessler is a retired high school counselor and produced playwright from Cottage Grove. "I love writing poetry because you have to make all of your words count to paint the picture you see in your mind."

. . . .

Elaine Kost

Elaine Kost lives in the beautiful Rogue Valley area of Southern Oregon. She lived in Junction City up until a little over a year ago and wrote a Sustainable Living column for what was then the *Tri County Tribune*.

A homesteader by nature, she and her husband, grow a large majority of the food they eat and try to purchase local when they can. She enjoys crafts of all kinds including spinning, knitting, crochet, beading and hardanger.

Elaine sees writing as a way of expressing one's self as well as sharing knowledge. "I encourage everyone to try it as we all have something to say!"

. . . .

Hayden Larsen

Hayden Larsen, a 2012 graduate of Crow High School, is currently a student at Lane Community College working on getting a degree in Media Arts in order to fulfill his dream of becoming a motion picture director.

"I am also an amateur game developer and am currently working on several games. I first became interested in writing after finishing several high-school writing assignments where my love for old and classic horror ad monster movies influenced me. It's genre I specialize in. I am the creator of the literary horror character Jack and his website "Legend of Jack," and I am currently working on a PC game adaption on one of my stories featuring Jack called *The Nightmare of Samuel Ward*."

Abraham Lawrence

Abraham Lawrence is thirteen years old. He loves animals and enjoys biking, swimming and ice skating. He is interested in many things including science and technology. He also greatly enjoyed the Rural Arts Annual Movie Camp, and wishes to thank all who participated and made it possible.

. . . .

Muriel Linder

Muriel (Ava) Linder lives with her family in Elmira, Oregon. She spent many years studying Native American history, especially that related to the Cheyenne tribe, before writing "The White Man's Brother."

"I had written numerous magazine articles and newspaper items until that time, but working with fiction was a whole new ballgame. I loved bringing my characters to life!"

"White Man's Brother" is the first of these two books. Look for "The Rainbow Chasers, a sequel to WMB, which will be published in late 2015 by *Groundwaters* Publishing, LLC.

. . . .

Demetri Liontos

Demetri Liontos is a long-time Eugene resident and writer/poet. Formerly an English-as-a-Second Language teacher at Lane Community College and the University of Oregon, he is now devoting time in his retirement to writing more stories, poems and short plays. His passion for foreign travel has over decades given him a myriad of rich cultural experiences, in addition to learning five languages with which to liven up the entertaining that he and wife Claudia enjoy sharing. He is a life member of the Very Little Theatre, a passable cook, raconteur, hiker and a strong believer in local literary publications such as *Groundwaters.*

Liath MacTire

Liath MacTire calls himself a retired geezer who is doggedly evolving into curmudgeonhood. The evolving is a challenging process but an enjoyable one for everyone except those folk in close proximity who can and have been wounded by flying profanity. He does not, contrary to rumors, drink Devil's Club tea. The tea is a mild hallucinogen, and he does not need to be any odder.

. . . .

Norm Maxwell

Norm Maxwell is a maverick, there's no doubt about that; but, he's a maverick with a heart. His writing is rough and he calls it "drivel," and more recently "verbal vomit," but there is an innate kindness and caring that lies below the surface where he hopes to keep it hidden. He's always there for his neighbors in Lorane, whether they are in need of some firewood to keep their homes warm in the winters; or if they need some help building a fence or tilling their garden, he always finds time to be there. He loves animals and gives them names like "Michael Gray Fox." He tells his stories with a gruff poignance that touches the heart. He didn't want to write a bio, because he doesn't like to showcase himself, so I'm writing it for him. Be sure to read Norm's story, "Joey." He's a true hero 'round these parts! pe

. . . .

Jim Miller

I was born and raised in Southern California. My wife Glenda and I were married in San Angelo, Texas in 1970, while I was training with the Air Force. After I served as a Vietnamese linguist overseas, Glenda and I moved to Bend, Oregon in 1973. I completed my English BA degree in 2005, and have taught for 17 years. I am currently a tour guide for school kids traveling to Washington, DC. I love to be with kids and see them capture and appreciate new *insights and observations. The highlight of my life has been to stand at the Lincoln Memorial, look back at the Washington Monument and the Capitol, pinch myself and say, "Wow, I get to do this everyday!"*

Jeanette-Marie Mirich

An Oregonian by birth, Jeanette-Marie Mirich graduated with a B.S. degree in education from Portland State University. She married her college sweetheart and began a peripatetic lifestyle courtesy of the U.S. Air Force and her husband's medical training. She packed up the kids and lived from Texas to Thailand, with 27 years living along the western shore of Lake Michigan. Passionate about needs in the third world, she accompanied her husband on many trips while he used his surgical techniques in Kenya, Ethiopia, Nicaragua, and Mali. She scribbles poems or short stories on notebooks, ruled and unruled paper or napkins. Grammy to 13 exceptional grandchildren, she travels from Kentucky through Kansas to the Pacific Northwest writing stories, making brownies and quilting. She winters in Kentucky and enjoys Oregon summers.

Barbara Newman

Barbara Newman was born in NYC. Raised by first generation immigrants, she learned much about their old country. While attending elementary school she felt strangely different from those other American children; memorizing past presidents in social studies, never made sense to her. When she was home with her parents, they talked in their native tongue and read about princesses, kings and past monarchies. Strangely foreign herself, Barbara proceeded through school and life, visiting her foster parents' homeland frequently. She found herself at home along with her returning elders. Barbara now lives in Sweden 6 months of the year.

Tom Oroyan

Thomas Oroyan, originally from Waimanalo, Hawaii, is an architect who retired in 2011. He now enjoys writing and taking classes at the Campbell Senior Center where his wife, gael Doyle-Oroyan, teaches a memoir-writing class.

Brian Palmer

Brian Palmer was raised in the small towns and woods of western Oregon, where he learned solitude and writing. He grew up not in the lap of luxury, but in the lap of wonderful, loving parents and three great brothers. After high school (go Falcons!) Brian served in the US Navy before returning to the West Coast and working 20 years as an electrician and in sales. In between was a falling away from the faith and virtues that had served him in his youth and he was nearly murdered for his efforts inside a ratty trailer house in Bakersfield, California. "Four Black Crows" and "Leroy's Christmas Eve" are poems in Brian's memoir of poetry and short stories, *Faith and Crossroads* that is available on Amazon.com.

. . . .

Rachel Rich

My memoir, *What Next?!*, covers birth to present. Life began as a grand adventure moving from place to place in a 28-foot trailer. Dad laid the first gas pipelines in the Pacific Northwest while Mom feverishly cooked, sewed and home-schooled our way into civilization. With my folks and grandfolks, we entertained ourselves by reading aloud and discussing far-out topics, especially... "On a Dark and Stormy Night."

. . . .

Doug Russell

I finished my school years in Oakridge where I spent more time hiking trails and fishing rivers and lakes than paying attention to teachers and blackboards. However, it was a reading out loud by a brave teacher of "The Rime of the Ancient Mariner" that sparked my interest in poetry. It took 45 years for the seed to bloom. I have worked at many different jobs including commercial fishing in Alaska and a tour of Vietnam, compliments of the U.S. Army. My wife Dot and I have a wonderful family with 4 kids, 12 grandkids and 4 great-grandkids.

Vicki Sourdry

Vicki has been writing, mostly science fiction, since 1985 when she picked up a thunderegg in Eastern Oregon and thought it looked like the map of a planet. She set about writing a book about that planet, and has been writing, off and on, ever since. She enjoys making up universes that can be populated by characters of her own design. She lives in Lane County.

. . . .

Jessie Schlaser Stinson

Jessie Stinson resides in Astoria Oregon where she grew up. She has two children, four grandchildren and many great grandchildren.

Jessie loves God, nature, flowers, gardening and writing. She writes of what she loves and sincerely shares her experiences with God and the miracles he has shown her. She has a deep desire to help others find God as she has.

Jessie pubished a book of her poems called *Grandma's Road to Inspiration* under the name of Jessie Schlaser and shares it with others in her prisoner outreach program with which she has been active for many years..

. . . .

Janice Strupp

I have always liked to write. I was a dedicated diarist in my teen-age years and have been an equally faithful chronicler of my world travels as an adult. I feel most alive and engaged with myself and the world when I am writing my response to an event or situation or memory. My journalist experience was with *The Springfield News* and *Northwest Boomer & Senior News*. I was also fortunate to be able to share my love of words and language as an English instructor at Pioneer Pacific College in Springfield.

Christine Thom

Christine is a fifteen year old who lives on a small farm in Oregon. She has done livestock 4-H for six years, and she enjoys photography, piano, working with farm animals, and spending time with family.

. . . .

Susanne Twight-Alexander

Susanne Twight-Alexander was raised in California State Parks where her father was a ranger; and lived 25 years in Trinity County, where her three children were born. She enjoys hiking, photography, biking, writing (one chapbook Being), maintaining her blog (http:www.susyouzel.com) and grandchildren. She and her husband have lived in Eugene, Oregon for 26 years.

. . . .

Terah Van Dusen

Terah Van Dusen is a poet and aspiring memoirist living in Elmira, Oregon with her boyfriend who works on a local organic farm. She loves to read and write personal stories, essays and poems.

Terah manages the post office in Alvadore, Oregon and is a former park ranger and counselor for incarcerated youth. She is a graduate of Northern Arizona University and is originally from Del Norte County in Northern California.

Aside from sorting mail and getting to know locals at the post office, she is also focusing on her writing career and hopes to publish the memoir about growing up with her father off-the-grid in Northern California. You can read her blog at terah-vandusen.wordpress.com. She also has a book of poetry out, titled *Love, Blues, Balance* for sale via her blog or on Amazon.com

Ron Veneski

Ron Veneski was born in Pennsylvania. After high school he joined the Navy and served on aircraft carriers as an electrician's mate. He was fortunate to visit France, Spain, Greece and Italy during his tour of duty. After the Navy, Ron earned a BA in Biology from San Jose State University. Upon graduating, he spent several years working for the California State Health Department. Deciding to become a teacher, Ron got his Master's Degree in Biology and a teaching certificate from California State University-Sacramento. He taught high school science in California for 10 years. Then, in 1980, he, his wife and son moved to Oregon where he taught high school science at McKenzie High School (Blue River) for 20 years. Ron and his wife have raised Alpacas for 19 years on their alpaca ranch in Eugene. Their son, daughter-in-law, and grandson live in Portland.

. . . .

Erik Wahl

Erik Wahl aka The BrainPoet has been helping keep Eugene weird for the past 7 years. He is a practicing Autist and member of KindTree.

His other interests include geometry, numerology, and digital art.

. . . .

Karen Wickham

Karen is a transplant from Dallas, Texas, coming to Oregon 16 years ago in search of trees. Later in life she is discovering her voice in essays, memoirs and poetry, saying what only she can say. She lives on 1½ acres of Veneta, Oregon paradise with her beloved life partner Dean, 8 chickens and a very exceptional dog, Bhakti. She is mother to three and grandmother to 6 awesome little people, her greatest joy is hanging out with family. Of late her mother-heart is opening to the whole human family, understanding that we are all the same in different flavors, struggling through this life adventure together.

FROM THE BOOKSHELF

In this segment, we are listing some of the more recent books produced by authors and poets who have published their work in *Groundwaters* over the years. We hope that you will take time to read those that interest you and support our local writers!

~~*~*~*~*~*

S.O.S. ~ Songs Of Sobriety ~ A Personal Journey Of Recovery by C.S. Blue (April 2013)

Over 20 years in the making, Songs Of Sobriety chronicles the first ten years in the recovery process, from newcomer to a strong foundation and new-found strength in dealing with life's problems. In this groundbreaking book, California/Oregon poet C. Steven Blue is a great source of inspiration, not only for those in recovery, but for anyone seeking to help themselves or someone else with the every day difficulties that life throws our way.

Inspirational and revealing, the book channels the struggles, the emotions and the healing processes of recovery, in linear story fashion, in verse. With over 25 years in recovery, C. Steven Blue's own experiences and observations serve as the basis for this moving book, filled with the wonder and renewal that recovery brings.

"Enter C. S. Blue's S.O.S Songs of Sobriety and step onto a remarkable rescue boat of poems chronicling his journey to recovery from addiction. Follow the poet's frank accounts of acute distress, his discovery of a life raft (H.P., Love) and crucial keys for lifting himself out of the mire in the first ten years of that recovery. Blue's poems will resonate with those who have endured epic loneliness and isolation. "Chair Dreams" is an anthem to the utter stasis of certain conditions before help is sought or accepted.

"Section by section, Blue rocks the reader forward in a personal cadence. Rhyme, slant rhyme, riffs of language and mantra appear in free form and in poignant refrains. Most lives get battered one way or another. Blue's S.O.S. collection gives readers in recovery of any kind one form of playbook, one person rescued, tapping out joy in fresh ability to feel, work, love – small joys, finally accepted and allowed." By Q.H.

Also... *Black Tights* (2013) and *Word Songs* (1992)

My Time in Paradise by Michael J. Barker (November 2014)

Hoss Barker may be a self-proclaimed redneck who spent his younger adult years working in the rough and tumble logging industry in the backwoods of Oregon, but he is also a poet in the truest sense of the word. Hoss' poetry is scattered throughout this book and when he dons his poet's hat, the words flow from his heart and soul. His poetry speaks of his deep love and respect for Mother Nature's creations, whether they be the rivers, trees and mountains or the many and varied types of wildlife that he enjoyed while spending six years at the Paradise Lodge in the wild and scenic section of the Rogue River – Zane Grey Country!

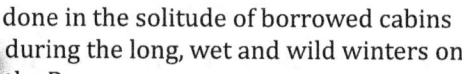

Hoss took the job at Paradise so that he could write his poetry while communing with Mother Nature and all of her wonders. While there, he published three books of poetry and prose. *My Time in Paradise* is Hoss' story of those six years spent in the wilderness that he loved. There was little time during the tourist season when he could write, so most of it was done in the solitude of borrowed cabins during the long, wet and wild winters on the Rogue.

One of the main parts of his job at the lodge during tourist season was overseeing the work of the temporary crew members that "The Boss" brought upriver to work each spring and summer. With much humor and a bit more exasperation, Hoss tells of the difficulties and adventures that were presented to him as he wrangled his "herd" of Meatheads. He struggled to learn to be a little more tolerant, but it was not easy for a former logger who was used to giving an honest day of hard work for his pay... who had a work ethic that would not tolerate laziness or carelessness. There was no such thing as "political correctness" in the woods. Either you did the job or you "hiked er." In the process, however, after dozens of "sensitivity lectures" from The Boss and The Boss Lady, he began to realize that maybe, in truth, he was the biggest Meathead of them all.

The Ballads of Lewis and Clark by *Michael J. Barker (May 2013)*

Two hundred years ago, a group of hardy frontiersmen set out from St. Louis, Missouri, and headed west under orders from President Thomas Jefferson to find the Northwest Passage and open up the newly-acquired Louisiana Purchase Territory. The adventure is still celebrated with all the zeal as it was in the days of yore. Come along on the trip with Oregon wilderness poet and retired logger, Michael J. "Hoss" Barker, and partake of the festivities from the comfort of your own easy chair.

OREGON'S MAIN STREET: U.S. Highway 99 "The Stories" by Jo-Brew (2013)

Long before Interstate 5 was built, Pacific Highway, later designated U.S. Highway 99, became our "Main Street" not only through the State of Oregon, but from Mexico to Canada. Unlike I-5, U.S. Highway 99 went through towns and small communities along its path, bringing them the means to connect with the rest of the state and nation.

OREGON'S MAIN STREET: U.S. Highway 99 "The Stories" takes us along this route today, but it is filled with the stories of those who grew up, worked, played and raised their families in the communities along its path. Over 150 individuals shared their stories, some in the form of old letters and diaries, but most in first-person accounts through interviews, letters, email and even phone calls all done personally by Jo-Brew.

"Oregon's Main Street is a very interesting collection of local histories, personal anecdotes, and descriptions of roadside attractions hung together like beads on the string of a trip up Highway 99. It was entertaining, and I came away with a list of places I want to visit. I've driven past some of them a hundred times without discovering them myself." By V.D.B.

OREGON'S MAIN STREET: U.S. Highway 99 "The Folk History" by Jo-Brew and Pat Edwards (September 2014)

In 1913, the first shovelful of dirt was turned by Oregon Governor Oswald West on the Siskiyou Pass to mark the beginning of the construction of the long-dreamed-of Pacific Highway through Oregon. At the time, the whole State of Oregon had only 25 miles of paved road. Even after construction of the highway had begun, it was mainly dirt and gravel for quite some time. Federal money did not pour into the project until 1921. Up to that time, it was up to the individual counties along the route to come up with the funding to build the roads through each of their areas. By its completion in 1926, however, it was adopted as U.S. Highway 99 and was declared the longest improved highway in the country by 1928. Actually, the history of the highway began long before 1913. This book will cover how the route for the Pacific Highway was determined through its use by Native tribes and later by trappers, miners and settlers who used portions of the California and Applegate Trails in their journeys, and eventually by the stage lines and the railroad. It will also show how each of the settlements along its route were formed and grew into prospering cities, small rural communities and some that are now ghost towns. Join us on our journey through these communities as we wend our way north from the California border where the Pacific Highway first started from that shovelful of dirt. You'll learn about some of the interesting, but lesser-known, aspects of their histories and the people who were instrumental in making them what they are today.

"I loved this book! The intersection of personal history and fact is seamless, and it makes the region come alive. The photographs, especially, draw you in to each interesting segment. I recommend it not only to those who want to know about the history of the places mentioned, but the way that small and large-town American life evolved as the highway did. Well done." by Amazon reader

The Self-Advocacy Toolbox: Advocate, Educate and Illuminate Your Life by Jennifer B. Chambers (June 2014)

A workbook for promoting self-advocacy as a means to being happier and living a more fulfilled life.

Brambleberry Farm (Maple Grove Chronicles) by Jennifer Chambers (June 19, 2013)

Brambleberry Farm is a place where friends become family through a shared love of sustainable living and good food. It follows Jo, a chef at the organic restaurant on site, who also has synesthesia, a disease where she experiences two sensations at the same time.

Remarkable Oregon Women by Jennifer Chambers (November 2015)   **NEW!**

Without the efforts of inspiring, brave women of the past, the progressive and individualistic Oregon we know today might not exist. From native tribes and Oregon Trail pioneers to Victorian suffragists and unlikely politicians, strong female leaders give profound meaning to the state motto, *alis volat propriis*—she flies with her own wings

. . . .

Turds in Your Teacup?: It's Been One of Those Days! by Gene Conrad (October 2015)

From time to time, all of us experience days or events that don't quite go as expected – and that is definitely good news! Those surprises can do anything from just making our eyebrows go up to providing a life lesson that adjusts our perspective in significant ways. Sharing stories of the twists and turns we encounter in life brings us together by helping us to see what shapes us into who we are. It is my hope that this book will encourage you to share your stories with your important people.

NEW!

Superfluous Women (22nd Daisy Dalrymple mystery) by Carola Dunn (06/09/15)

NEW!

After World War I, Britain's loss of two million young men meant that many young women would never have the chance to marry. Some called them spinsters or old maids, but the press called them surplus or superfluous. Superfluous Women, Carola Dunn's 22nd mystery in the Daisy Dalrymple series, is the first novel I have read to address this issue in history. Interestingly, being superfluous freed some women from the restrictions of societal roles, allowing them to make their own lives and fortunes in the world...

Valley of the Shadow (Cornish mystery series) by Carola Dunn (12/11/2012)

A cryptic message spurs Eleanor, Megan, and Nick Gresham on a frantic search for a refugee's missing family

. . . .

White Fist & Two Dogs by David R.L. Erickson (June 2014)

Beyond an incomprehensible boundary, separated from the seemingly infinite omniverse, lies Hevn, a tabletop world alone in a deep, starless dark. Upon its face a complex array of contrasting, often violently incompatible physics and cultures abide. Only a handful of beings share the truth of its creation and purpose. Significant among them is Shiric, the architect of the world and currently a prisoner upon it, albeit one who continues to wield a mighty technology, exerting God-like influence over his construct. Another is his adversary, The Fayne, who has been tasked with bringing order to a chaotic environment while insuring Shiric's imprisonment remains uninterrupted.

"I relish a good science fiction/fantasy epic. ... On one hand, Hevn and its inhabitants are strange and alien with technologies and powers that are so fantastic they border on the magical ... yet the characters of Narregan (White Fist) and his guardian Brin, who are of an elite warrior caste ... convey enough familiar human/earth-like themes that I am kept wondering what the connection to our own universe/world might be. The other side of the story takes place in the 1870s of the American southwest with an immediately likeable character, Jonas Two Dogs, who has a power of his own ... Both of these worlds meet when Narregan and Brin's mission on Hevn sweeps them into Jonas' world and their paths intertwine on a journey of violent horror and spiritual wonder."

Wakanisha Is Love Enough by Michael Foster (2014)

To the Lakota Sioux, the word Wakanisha roughly translates as children, but has a far deeper meaning. Wakanisha are their sacred vessels of culture, spirituality and most importantly, love. These first inhabitants of America strived for harmony in all things, with the land of rolling plains they freely roamed, and within their tribes, families, and hearts. Follow three generations of these remarkable people as their daily lives paint a beautiful and bittersweet picture, the threads of their canvas interwoven with our country's troublingly real history.

"Mouse has become a good friend and teacher to me. The story is sad - it's always been sad - but the fascinating details of Native American life revealed in this story, and the author's obvious love for the subject matter, made this book a joy to read. Mr. Foster knows his material and is close to it. A beautiful story for anyone interested in the lives of those who owned this land before the white man arrived. Excellent read." By C.K.

. . . .

Building a Better Nest: Living Lightly at Home and in the World by Evelyn Hess (June 2015)   **NEW!**

For fifteen years, Evelyn Hess and her husband David lived in a tent and trailer, without electricity or running water, on twenty acres of wild land in the foothills of the Oregon Coast Range. When they decided to build a house, they knew it would have to respect the lessons of simple living that they learned in their camping life. *Building a Better Nest* chronicles their adventures as they begin to construct a house of their own, seeking a model for sustainable living not just in their home, but beyond its walls.

ALSO...
To the Woods: Sinking Roots, Living Lightly, and Finding True Home by Evelyn Hess (May 2010)

To the Woods is the true story of that 15 years spent in a tent and trailer. *To the Woods* describes Evelyn's day-to-day struggles, failures, and discoveries. It tracks the natural history of place through the seasons. It wrestles with issues like human impact on the ecology of our planet.

"Evelyn Hess writes 'Never ever do we want to take the Earth's offerings for granted.' Evelyn and David Hess put their city lives on hold, purchased twenty-one wooded acres in the Oregon Coast Range foothills, and developed a wild plant nursery while planning their new home and a life bent on the learning and living with the joys in their surrounding natural environment. For any natural history buff, and those of us who care about keeping this green earth intact for future generations, To the Woods is a beautifully written must read. Let's hope to hear more from Hess's green world." by Patty

Steps in Life by Roy K. Johnston (2014)

R. K. Johnston is an international poet recognized in the field of cultural integration, creativity, and the unity of knowledge. His poetry is infused with the music and rhythm of a career classical and jazz performer. Recently he has been a featured reader in Croatia; Portugal; Madhopur, India; Kingston, Jamaica; and Portland and Eugene, Oregon.

"Roy K. Johnston is a 21st century renaissance man whose intellectual curiosity takes him on a wandering journey through many disciplines and experiences, where asking questions and observing cultures, circles him back to a sense of the universe and the present." - Jerry Smith, Poet, San Luis Obispo, CA

. . . .

The White Man's Brother by Muriel Linder (May 2015)

The mesmerizing story of Fire Top, the red-haired white brave who came to live with Tall Bear and Quiet Woman in their Cheyenne village after his birth parents were killed by members of another tribe. Muriel Linder brings her characters to life and Fire Top's story will allow the reader to share in life as it was lived among the Cheyenne tribe in the mid-1800s. Follow the stories of Fire Top's love for Moon Wolf and Shining Eyes; his hatred for Big Calf; and his friendship and relationships with the white frontiersmen with whom the tribe lived in peace.

"Muriel Linder's book, The White Man's Brother, is a delightful must read for children and adults alike, who are seeking insight and understanding into the culture and heritage of early Northwest America. The history and cultural lessons are wrapped up in a fast paced adventure story that keeps you enthralled from chapter to chapter... Each chapter coaxes the reader on to the next, making it a hard book to set down. The story begs for a sequel." by S.H.

. . . .

Happy Christmas, Miss Lawrence by Jeanette-Marie Mirich (Sept 2013)

Join Missionary, Alexandra Lawrence, and Jockey, Robin Huntington, as they race to solve the mystery of her arrest, allowing her to make it home for Christmas - the truth may set her free, but will it destroy the promise of love?

"I haven't been this delighted while reading a book in a long time. Not that I haven't enjoyed the books I've been reading, but wow. I felt like a guest within the story, as if I was sitting on the sofa while all the real-to-life, loveable characters were living their lives in front of me. (It is) set in England at Christmastime, while horses race through frigid fields, and legal mix-ups lock the characters in close proximity..." by C.C.

This book just won second place in the Colorado Independent Publishers Association EVVY award in Fiction/Romance Category.

Faith and Crossroads by Robert Brian Palmer (December 2013)

Told through colorful characters, author Robert Brian Palmer cleverly weaves his testimony throughout short-stories and poems that record the journey of a man struggling on the brink of destruction and finds himself faced with the decision of falling into the abyss or returning to a loving Savior.

"With some real life experiences, short stories that keep you in suspense and poems that have deep thought and meaning, this book keeps your interest. It can be read quickly or spend some time in thought as you read." By R.K.

. . . .

Grandma's Road to Inspiration by Jessie Schlaser (October 2013)

Inspirational Poetry and Essays. 68 pages. Published by *Groundwaters* Publishing, LLC.

Jessie has a new book called *Fly Like and Eagle* coming out by early 2016.

https://www.createspace.com/4479531

. . . .

Being by Susanne Twight-Alexander (November 2012)

From the Klamath River to the Pacific Ocean and from the Trinity Alps Wilderness to the Cascades, Susanne Twight-Alexander's poems evolve from growing up in California State Parks and from years of hiking and backpacking as an adult. Her deep relationship with her natural surroundings is apparent in these poems. Illustrator Bella Peralta is an acclaimed artist working mainly in the disciplines of painting, weaving, printmaking and illustration. Being was originally published by *Groundwaters* Publishing, LLC in Lorane, Oregon.

"Being has the rare gift of an authentic poetic voice. Every poem describes a passionate engagement with each moment and an observation of the human condition. Twight-Alexander has crafted her poems with the spare truth of a real life. We feel her hiking the wilderness and dealing with relationships as if we were by her side. Peralta's art work adds another wonderful component to this chapbook. Don't overlook this special opportunity to read a new poetic voice." By B.W.F.

Love, Blues, Balance by Terah Van Dusen (December 2014)

A thoughtful assembly of poems by an aspiring memoirist. Exploring these three themes: Love, Blues and Balance, the author finds it impossible to conceal her truest feelings. With each section revealing unique perspectives on the subjects of love and attachment, the author's recounts are well worth the read.

"So incredibly thrilled to see this book for sale, written by one of the most talented, beautiful souls I have ever known. Thank you so much, Terah" by K.M.

Photo Gallery

Construction of McArthur Court. From the Guide to the Ellis Fuller Lawrence Papers, Northwest Digital Archives, http://nwda-db.wsulibs.wsu.edu/findaid/ark:/80444/xv35243

Guidelines for 2016 Annual Issue

1. Email submissions are preferred. Copy text into the body of an email message or MS-Word or WordPerfect file attachments, please; no headers, footers, or in-line graphics.
2. Include a phone number or email address with each submission. You may use a pseudonym, but all work must be signed.
3. Submission limit is 2,000 words for prose; no more than 2 poems unless they are very short.
4. Please be respectful to all. Read *Groundwaters* to understand its audience, and speak from the heart. Every age is welcome here. Featured artists and authors are representative of all ages and levels of experience. We do not accept political or religious opinion pieces and we ask our submitters to limit the use of profanity to only what the story requires. No explicit sexual content or unnecessary violence will be accepted. The editors reserve the right to edit the unacceptable if it is to be published.
5. Include a bit of information about yourself and your submission to share with our readers.
6. Original works are protected under the copyright of *Groundwaters* and may not be reproduced without permission of the author/artist. They remain the property of the author/artist.
7. Works in the public domain may be submitted to reprint, but credits to authors/artists must be included.
8. Changes may be made in submitted material due to grammatical errors and space constraints. Whenever possible, the material and content will not be altered.
9. Contributing authors and poets will be offered a 40% discount from the retail price of the book. Contact Pat Edwards, contact@groundwaterspublishing.com, for information on how to obtain your discount for on-line orders.

DEADLINE FOR SUBMITTING MATERIAL TO

Groundwaters 2016:

August 15, 2016

This book has been produced by *Groundwaters* Publishing, LLC by volunteer staff members:

Pat Edwards
Jennifer Chambers
Patrice Broome
Jim Burnett Sr.

. . . .

For on-line orders, go to our eStore:
https://www.createspace.com/5709844

To order books directly from the publishers, please contact:

Pat Edwards, Managing Editor
Groundwaters Publishing, LLC
P.O. Box 50
Lorane, OR 97451
contact@groundwaterspublishing.com
http://groundwaterspublishing.com